WILDSAM

"I've heard entertainers and producers
tell me that we got some kind of
sound here they can't get anywhere else."
—*Percy Sledge,* Muscle Shoals

WILDSAM PURSUITS

Places are endlessly complex: time, geography, culture and happenings layered with millions of stories. And often, one realizes that a place carries a specific heritage, a definitive pursuit that people build their lives around, a common trade or precious resource that might set the course for generations.

For Alabama, this pursuit is music.

Our thanks to the medley of folks who helped us take our love for Alabama to record heights. Traci Thomas offered early ideas and contacts. Melany Robinson and the Sprouthouse team pointed our research in fun directions as did Sara Camp Arnold, Parker Duffey, Maria Ivey, Dana Wade, Caleb Johnson, Lisa Cericola and Annemarie Anderson. Thanks also to Sara Lewis, Christine Strauder and Kate McMullen. This book would not exist without the local knowledge of our fabulous contributors and the folks who shared their stories in interviews, essays and poetry. All our respect and gratitude to the historians, writers and artists telling true stories of this complex and beautiful place.

WILDSAM FIELD GUIDES™

Copyright © 2023

All rights reserved. No portion of this
book may be reproduced in any form without
permission from the publisher.

Published in the United States
by Wildsam Field Guides, Austin, Texas.

"Sam Cooke Sings to Me When I Am Afraid" and "God Speaks to Alabama" reprinted from *Magic City Gospel* Copyright ©2017 by Ashley M. Jones. Used with permission of the publisher, Hub City Press. All rights reserved.

ISBN 978-1-4671-9991-9

Illustrations by Josh Carnley

To find more field guides, please visit
www.wildsam.com

CONTENTS

Discover the people and places that tell the story of Alabama

WELCOME

WHEN YOU CREST LOOKOUT MOUNTAIN, the green highway sign says "Welcome to Alabama the Beautiful." It's a simple slogan, one any state could use. But if you travel southward toward the red-clay country beyond, Alabama makes good on that claim in unexpected ways.

The landscape sways from the cool depths of Cathedral Caverns to piney thickets around Talladega to a glittering coast, making Alabama one of the nation's most biologically diverse states. The Black Warrior and the Cahaba thread toward the sea; bay-breasted warblers swap out colors like seasonal kaleidoscopes. Now and again, extraordinary phenomena occur. In 1833, the Leonid meteor shower rained light on a November night, and. almost 200 years later, the phrase "Stars Fell on Alabama" still echoes.

Such mysteries unfold here. Time passes. New meanings and inspirations emerge. At Gee's Bend, generations of quilters turn a craft driven by household necessity into explosive, even radical art. Not far away in the Black Belt, the Rural Studio's architecture responds to need with ingenuity and gritty commitment. The photographer William Christenberry turns his camera into a capsule of Hale County textures. A young woman from Monroeville, working odd jobs in New York City, coaxes small-town intimacies and injustice into *To Kill a Mockingbird*.

The Yuchi people call the Tennessee River "the Singing River," and the musical ecosystem has lured artists here, from Aretha to Bono. One of them, Steve Winwood, observed: "Somehow music can reflect landscapes." The Alabama sound takes many forms, among them the country-tinged high lonesome of Percy Sledge. He first sang while working in the fields. Later, he belted a number one soul hit, "When a Man Loves a Woman," with a multiracial Muscle Shoals band that defied a segregated time.

The lawyer and activist Bryan Stevenson told us something about Alabama: "It's a place where the opportunity for restoration and change is rich." He helped found Montgomery's National Memorial for Peace and Justice, which sears heart and mind as it reckons with racial terror and lynching. Everything about that place and this state tells us that what Bryan Stevenson said is true: Alabama's beauty is anything but simple. It's as complex as bonds between people across time, enduring as the soil they walk. —The Editors

SELECTED CONTENT

ESSENTIALS

Trusted intel and travel info about iconic culture, geography and entry points to the traditions and landscapes of Alabama

PLANNING

TRANSPORT

TRAIN

Crescent [New Orleans to NYC]
Hop on at three Alabama stops.
amtrak.com

BIKE

Redemptive Cycles
New/used bikes, mechanic classes, public work station.
redemptivecycles.com

LANDMARKS

EDMUND PETTUS BRIDGE

Alabama River, Selma
Site of Bloody Sunday, national symbol of fight for civil rights.

SLOSS FURNACES

20 32nd St N, Birmingham
Repurposed iron plant represents 1890s shift from ag to industry.

MEDIA

RADIO

Alabama Public Radio
Bama Bluegrass Saturday nights.

Birmingham Mountain Radio
Local Mash on Sundays showcases Magic City music.

ONLINE NEWS

AL.com
Two Pulitzers in 2023, including a team with father-son journalists John and Ramsey Archibald.

CLIMATE

Ramble down Alabama and you'll pass from cool Appalachian air to warm coastal breezes. Abundant sunshine and rainfall allow for a long growing season [up to 300 days] and boost the state's top rank for biodiversity east of the Mississippi. Yes, it's subject to nature's wicked side too, with a coast vulnerable to hurricanes and tornado threats farther north. Temps can crack 100 degrees; winters can bring a snow or two. Meanwhile, Loop Current in the Gulf ushers up tropical waters. Water vapor falls as rain, keeping this desert latitude lush.

CALENDAR

JAN	Von Brewski Beer Fest
FEB	Mardi Gras in Mobile
MAR	Spring Gulf fishing [cobia, pompano, bluefish]
APR	*To Kill a Mockingbird* at Monroeville courthouse
MAY	CoalFest
JUN	Peach Jam Jubilee
JUL	W.C. Handy Music Fest
AUG	Black Belt Folk Roots Festival
SEP	AL Women in Jazz Fest
OCT	Kentuck Festival of Arts Old Time Fiddlers Fest
NOV	Iron Bowl
DEC	Bay Minette Christmas Festival

GEOGRAPHY

Notable terrain formations and where to find them.

HIGHLAND RIM
Hartselle sandstone is the main rock that forms this northwest/central ridge, with valleys made of limestone. *Florence, Decatur*

IMPACT CRATER
A star wound caused by a cosmic crash 80 million years go. One of six in the world. *Wetumpka Impact Crater*

BLACK BELT PRAIRIE
Crescent of dark, fertile soil curves into the state's lower half. Contrast to forests is visible from space. *Montgomery*

RED HILLS
Silt, sand, clay, marl, limestone compose rust-red crenellations across otherwise flat Coastal Plain. *Lake Eufaula*

STALAGMITE FOREST
Drippings from cave ceiling formed an underground forest of rock structures. *Cathedral Caverns*

FREE-FLOWING RIVER
Organic flow of water, free of dams, with a hospitable life habitat. Like a freshwater wilderness. *Cahaba River*

TRADITIONS

Tastes and traditions of Alabama that show culture, craft and history.

Barbecue	Legacy of pork cooked low and slow over open pits. Invention of mayo-based white sauce changed the game. *Big Bob Gibson Bar-B-Que, Decatur*
Football	Choose your chant: Roll Tide or War Eagle. College game rules here. *Iron Bowl, Tuscaloosa and Auburn*
Peaches	Georgia gets the attention, but Alabamians say their fruit is tops. Roadside stands hawk state's ag-tradition gem. *Peach Park, Clanton*
Protest	Rosa Parks, bus boycotts, marches, Freedom Rides. Ground zero for injustice *and* historic change. *Legacy Museum, Montgomery*
Quilting	In a state known for generational stitching skill, women of Gee's Bend are a most stunning expression. *Gee's Bend*

MUSIC SITES

A quick guide to recording and performing music spaces of Alabama.

FAME RECORDING STUDIOS
Capturing masterpieces like "Mustang Sally" since 1959.

MUSCLE SHOALS SOUND STUDIO
Where The Swampers laid it down in Sheffield.

THE NUTTHOUSE
Owned by former FAME engineer, Grammy winner.

WISHBONE RECORDING STUDIO
Part of the Shoals studio legacy since 1976.

DAUPHIN STREET SOUND
Two-studio operation making music out of Mobile.

SATURN
Outer-space-themed bar with local and touring acts.

THE ORION AMPHITHEATER
Huntsville's 8,000-seat outdoor venue, drawing national talent.

AVONDALE BREWING COMPANY
Brewery with top-notch outdoor stage setup.

THE NICK
Cold beer. Rock and roll.

STANDARD DELUXE
Rural Waverly, outside Auburn, always hosting a good time here with slew of indie acts.

CULTURAL INSTITUTIONS

KENTUCK ART CENTER & FESTIVAL

503 *Main Ave, Northport*

Rooted in folk art and with origins as a festival [est. 1971], the center offers year-round arts programming, from workshops to exhibits.

THE LEGACY MUSEUM: FROM ENSLAVEMENT TO MASS INCARCERATION

400 *N Court St, Montgomery*

A moving look at slavery and racial inequality in the U.S., with nearby National Memorial for Peace and Justice remembering victims of racial terror.

ALABAMA THEATRE

1817 *3rd Ave, Birmingham*

Illuminated by iconic blade sign, a showplace since 1927—from movie palace to live music and gold-leaf grandeur for ballet or symphony.

SCENIC DRIVES AND PUBLIC LANDS

Back roads and natural sites across the Yellowhammer State.

ALABAMA'S COASTAL CONNECTION

Loop around marshy Mobile Bay's fishing villages, breath in sea air from the docks of Bayou La Batre. Take the bridge to Dauphin Island for white sand, ferry on to Fort Morgan. *Grand Bay to Daphne*

CHEAHA STATE PARK

Oldest park in the state, since 1933, tucked into the Talladega National Forest at southern tip of the Appalachian mountains. Cheaha Mountain Trail leads to sweeping views atop Alabama's highest peak. *Delta*

THE APPALACHIAN HIGHLAND SCENIC BYWAY

Lush mountain landscapes make a backdrop for Little River Canyon's 600-foot cliffs. At Piedmont, cross Chief Ladiga Trail, a 33-mile trail along an old rail corridor. *Heflin to Fort Payne*

DESOTO STATE PARK

Wildflowers, woods and the cooling spray of 104-foot DeSoto Falls, among the tallest in the country. Hike the Laurel Falls or Lost Falls Trails loops at this Civilian Conservation Corps park. *Fort Payne*

TENSAW PARKWAY

Follow the river delta and drop into the coast at Mobile. The Alabama Coastal Birding Trail follows part of this route, with Blakeley State Park a stop for river tour. *Little River to Mobile*

OAK MOUNTAIN STATE PARK

Hike an old logging road under a canopy of green, thunder down single track on a mountain bike, meander the nature trail for bird-watching or take a cool dip in Double Oak Lake from the sandy beach. *Pelham*

BLACK BELT NATURE AND HERITAGE TRAIL

Cultural landmarks, from Gee's Bend to Tuskegee Institue, alongside nature's wonders. Spot red-eyed vireos at Chickasaw State Park. Stroll a ghost town at Old Cahawba Archaeological Park. Camp at Paul M. Grist State Park. *Selma to Tuskegee*

CULTURE

FILM

Selma
Forrest Gump
The Miracle Worker
Muscle Shoals
Capote
The Tuskegee Airmen
Big Fish
4 Little Girls
To Kill a Mockingbird
Talladega Nights
The Phenix City Story
Fried Green Tomatoes

MUSIC

Alabama Shakes
"Hold On"

Clarence Carter
"Patches"

Ella & Louis
"Stars Fell on Alabama"

Jason Isbell
"Alabama Pines"

Shelby Lynne
"Where I'm From"

BOOKS

☞ *Transcendent Kingdom* by Yaa Gyasi: Science meets religion in this story drawing on Gyasi's real life as Alabama daughter of Ghanaian immigrants.

☞ *Barracoon: The Story of the Last "Black Cargo"* by Zora Neale Hurston: Celebrated Alabama-born writer's 1927 interviews with Oluale Kossola [Cudjoe Lewis], a last-known survivor of Atlantic slave trade into Mobile.

☞ *South to America: A Journey Below the Mason-Dixon to Understand the Soul of a Nation* by Imani Perry: Birmingham-born writer returns to region in this sharp-eyed memoir/travelogue. National Book Award winner.

☞ *Lets Us Now Praise Famous Men* by James Agee: It began as a 1936 *Fortune* magazine assignment for Agee and photographer Walker Evans. It became an influential and poetic record in time of people and the land.

☞ *Big Fish: A Novel of Mythic Proportions* by Daniel Wallace: An Alabama son's quest to understand his father through a series of outragous tales.

☞ *Carry Me Home: Birmingham, Alabama, The Climactic Battle of the Civil Rights Revolution* by Diane McWhorter: Pulitzer-winning epic examines Klan rallies, church bombing and author's own family amid a movement.

ISSUES

Voting Rights — The march to Montgomery and eventual Voting Rights Act of 1965 is a consequential part of the state's legacy, no doubt. Unfortunately, barriers to limit votes remain, especially for Black, low-income or formerly incarcerated residents, among others. Groups like Alabama Arise work to enact pro-democracy policies. **EXPERT:** *Robyn Hyden, executive director, Alabama Arise*

Racial Injustice — Lack of investment in equitably distributed infrastructure, education, healthcare, is one of the factors contributing to ongoing racial injustice. Organizations like Alabama Appleseed work for policy change, systemic solutions. **EXPERT:** *Carla Crowder, executive director, Alabama Appleseed Center for Law & Justice*

Clean Waterways — Alabama is laced with rivers, streams and lakes, feeding its rich biodiversity, which also means care must be taken to keep waterways clean. This is a cause broad enough to unite people across organizations and the political spectrum. **EXPERT:** *Sam Howell, president Alabama Scenic River Trail*

Criminal Justice — Low-income Alabamians face a heavier toll in a system also fraught with racial disparity. Organizations like Equal Justice Initiative provide legal aid, educate about reform, work to overturn wrongful convictions, advocate for better prison conditions. **EXPERT:** *Bryan Stevenson, executive director, Equal Justice Initiative*

STATISTICS

75 ....Gold and platinum recordings associated with The Swampers
6,350 ....Species living in a biodiverse Alabama
11 ....Number of Crimson Tide undefeated seasons
1902 ....Year Alabamian Mary Anderson invented windshield wipers
15 million ....Pounds of peaches grown annually in Chilton County
600 feet ....Drop at Little River Canyon, the deepest in the East

SELECTED CONTENT

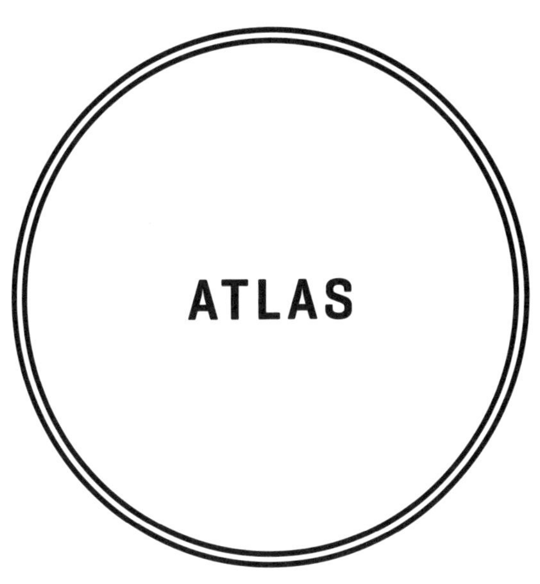

A guide to the sites and lands of the Yellowhammer State, including curated favorites, communities large and small, and a road trip through Alabama's past and present

BESTS

FOOD & DRINK

See our "meat and three" road trip itinerary on page 33.

NEW CLASSIC
Automatic Seafood
2824 5th Ave
Birmingham
Big hot-spot energy. Plates of Gulf oysters, tuna tartare, seasonal specials like blue crab or crawfish, all in homage to the coasts.

GULF CATCH
Fisher's
27075 Marina Rd
Orange Beach
Fresh-caught grouper, tasso-gravied shrimp over grits, as water laps marina.

MEAT & THREE
Eagle's Restaurant
2610 16th St N
Birmingham
Line snakes down sidewalk for pork chops, oxtails and steamtable sides.

GREEK
The Bright Star
304 19th St N
Bessemer
Greek-style Gulf snapper and steak carry on long family and immigrant restaurant tradition [since 1905].

WINE BAR
Golden Age Wine
2828 Culver Rd
Mountain Brook
Zingy sips, creamy brie, folds of prosciutto cured for 24 months.

BISTRO
Chez Fonfon
2007 11th Ave S
Birmingham
Beloved spot where South meets Paris. Sister restaurant, Bottega, also stellar.

BARBECUE
Big Bob Gibson Bar-B-Que
1715 6th Ave SE
Decatur
Pork sandos and home to white sauce: mayo-based zip for smoked fowl. Flown coop to big fame.

LOCAL SOURCES
Odette
120 N Court St
Florence
Farm fresh, minimal decor [hardwoods, brick]. Bartenders know locals by name.

BAKERY
Abadir's
Various
Greensboro
Chef Sarah Cole's smart pop-ups draw on Egyptian/Southern American roots.

SLAW DOG

Bunyan's Bar-B-Que
901 College St
Florence
Neon-red dog, hot mustard slaw, steamy bun wrapped tight as a tamale. Magic.

GARDEN-TO-TABLE

Acre
210 E Glenn Ave
Auburn
Lively space by campus, an acre of produce onsite.

CARAMEL CAKE

Dean's Cake House
402 Snowden Dr
Andalusia
Seven layers! Baked and iced by hand.

LAKE VIEW

SpringHouse
12 Benson Mill Rd
Alexander City
Warm stone-and-timber space with seasonal tastes.

KOREAN

Kalim Korean BBQ
5806 Woodmere Blvd
Montgomery
Auto manufacturing drew Korean folks, boosting beef bulgogi, jjambbong.

SOUL FOOD

Mary's Southern Cooking
3011 SpringHill Ave
Mobile
The coastal go-to for fried chicken, meatloaf, collards, yams.

MODERN SOUTH

Helen
4000 3rd Ave S
Birmingham
Downtown dining in 1920's-era building. Angel biscuits, cane syrup butter, a must.

PLATE LUNCH

Jefferson Country Store
26120 Hwy 28
Jefferson
Pit stop since 1957. Fried bologna.

CHARGRILLED OYSTERS

SOCU Southern Kitchen
455 Dauphin St
Mobile
Chef Erica Barrett's hometown homage.

CATFISH

Top O' the River
3330 McClellan Blvd
Anniston
Don't skip the cornbread and greens.

BAR EXPERIENCE

House of Found Objects
2205 2nd Ave N
Birmingham
Slip into Elvis suit, sip a cocktail. Part art immersion, part speakeasy. Total trip.

BREWERY

Straight to Ale
2610 Clinton Ave
Huntsville
Take a Chill Pils, the house pilsner, or Stout at the Devil?

LOCAL HAUNT

The Garage Bar
2304 10th Ter S
Birmingham
Like a leafy backyard hang; good beer and sandos. Cash only.

COFFEE

June
213 25th St N
Birmingham
Woodworking shop turned stylish small-batch coffee roaster.

IRISH BAR & VENUE

Callaghan's Irish Social Club
916 Charleston St
Mobile
Burgers and tunes.

LODGING

SOUTHERN QUEEN

The Grand Hotel
Fairhope
grand1847.com
On Mobile Bay since 1847. Now with 550 acres of golf, pools, spa, 36-slip marina.

RUSTIC MODERN

GunRunner Boutique Hotel
Florence
gunrunnerhotel.com
Ten suites, lush tones of brick, beams and hardwoods. Music on the rooftop.

ARCHITECTURAL PRIZE

Elyton Hotel
Birmingham
elytonhotel.com
Historic lobby in marble and brass, mod-style rooms.

NEWCOMER

Trilogy Hotel
Montgomery
trilogyhotelmontgomery.com
Downtown digs near Alabama River.

DOWNTOWN BOUTIQUE

The Alamite
Tuscaloosa
@thealamite
Newcomer co-owned by Coach Saban. Walking distance to stadium, naturally.

SEASIDE STAY

The Lodge at Gulf State Park
Gulf Shores
lodgeatgulfstatepark.com
Back after 14-year hiatus [former lodge was destroyed by Hurricane Ivan].

NEIGHBORHOOD CHIC

Grand Bohemian Hotel
Mountain Brook
Near botanical gardens, zoo.

MIDCENTURY CHARM

106 Jefferson
Huntsville
106jefferson.com
Downtown. Throwback design to the space race era.

COUNTRY STAY

Pursell Farms
Sylacauga
pursellfarms.com
Estate-style resort by Pursell family. Cottages, inn, golf, live music events.

TOWN BOUTIQUE

The Stricklin
Florence
thestricklin.com
Overlooking downtown Florence. A bustling Big Bad Breakfast in lobby.

ROOFTOP POOL

The Laurel
Auburn
laurelhotelandspa.com
Student training and luxury space via Auburn's hospitality management school.

HISTORIC SPOT

Redmont Hotel
Birmingham
redmonthotelbirmingham.com
Hank's last night: room 907, Jan. 1, 1953.

OUTDOORS

MOUNTAIN BIKE

Red Mountain Park
Birmingham
redmountainpark.org
Iron ore once veined this mountain; now, 16 miles of forested trails.

CAMP

Gulf State Park
Gulf Shores
alapark.com
About 30 miles of trails, some shaded with mossy live oaks, others along dunes.

PADDLE

Cypress Creek
Florence
outdooralabama.com
Wade-fish the upper, kayak the lower, from County Road 16 to Wildwood Park.

RUN/WALK

Railroad Park
Birmingham
railroadpark.org
Greenspace in heart of town: 19-acre "living room" and rec hub.

FLOAT

The Cold Hole
Magnolia Springs
Cool off in magical river waters. Then, to Jesse's Restaurant for fried green tomatoes with Gulf shrimp.

RAFTING

Montgomery Whitewater
Montgomery
montgomerywhitewater.com
Manmade waterways for paddlers with Class II to IV rapids.

WANDER

Sloss Furnaces
Birmingham
slossfurnaces.com
Learn iron-industry history on self-guided tour of massive furnace, built 1882.

BOATING

Wilson and Wheeler Lakes
Florence/Decatur
Lock passage to boat and fish both lakes.

SPELUNKING

Cathedral Caverns
Woodville
alapark.com
Stalagmite forest includes "Goliath," 45 feet tall, 243-foot circumference.

PLANTS

Birmingham Botanical Gardens
bbgardensr.org
24+ gardens showcase diverse flora from the region and beyond, azalea to spiderlily.

GHOST TOWN

Old Cahawba Archaeological Park
Orrville
cahawba.com
Longtime Indigenous town; first state capital. Layered in history.

MEDITATE

Wichahpi Wall
Florence
"Tom's Wall" pays Homage to Yuchi great-great-grand-mother's journey.

SHOPS

FARMERS' MARKET

The Market at Pepper Place

2829 2nd Ave S

Birmingham

Piles of produce and loaves in 100+ tents.

GENTLEMEN'S SUPPLY

Roosevelt & Co.

114 *Clinton Ave E*

Huntsville

Denim to tailored suits, leather goods. Barber onsite too.

PARTY PREP

Toomey's Mardi Gras

755 *McRae Ave*

Mobile

Accoutrement and beads galore—70,000 square feet!

COUNTRY STORE

Mentone Market

5872 *Hwy* 117

Mentone

Atop Lookout Mountain for 80 years. Hip firestarter kits, CCC-themed bandanas and picnic nibbles.

FOUND TREASURE

Unclaimed Baggage

509 *W Willow St*

Scottsboro

Where the contents of lost luggage goes to find another life.

FLY SHOP

Deep South Outfitters

4700 *Cahaba River Rd, Birmingham*

From trout to tarpon, they've got the goods. Flies, gear, various boats to get out there.

ROADSIDE FARMSTAND

The Peach Park

2300 *7th St*

South Clanton

Baskets of fresh peaches plus all their best uses [homemade ice cream, pies].

BOUTIQUE

Ex Voto Vintage

514 *Cloverdale Rd*

Montgomery

Apparel, distinctive jewelry designs with antique elements.

SPECIALTY GROCER

Mark's Mart

1022 *County Road* 44

Selma

Local fave since '78. Alabama orange rolls, Joyce's cheese straws.

FURNISHINGS

Charles Phillips Antiques

4505 *Laurendine Rd*

Theodore

Eight warehouses, carefully curated.

BONBONS & BARS

Chocolatá

701 *37th St S*

Birmingham

Chocolate charcuterie packaged like salami.

BOOKSTORES

Page & Palette

Fairhope

Auburn Oil Co.

Auburn

Little Professor, Thank You Books, Reed Books

Birmingham

Ernest & Hadley

Tuscaloosa

ARTISTS & MAKERS

To read more about folk artists, see page 109.

FASHION
Billy Reid
billyreid.com
Flagship shop, studio for co-ed fashion. More than a dozen locations across U.S.

NATURE
Sara Garden Armstrong
saragarden armstrong.net
Sculpture, paintings, books. Themes of water, time, change.

TEXTILES
Aaron Sanders Head
aaronsanders head.com
Hand-stitched panels, quilts drawing on family traditions of ag, art, storytelling.

EXPERIENTIAL SPACE
Kentuck Art Center
kentuck.org
Four gallery spaces showing art across cultures, backgrounds. Festival and programming too.

QUILTING
Gee's Bend Collective
soulsgrowndeep.org/gees-bend-quiltmakers
Ancestral art, revered nationwide.

PRINTMAKER
Debra Riffe
@tupelogal
Woodcut, linoleum block prints rendering Black experiences rooted in place and time.

POTTERY
Katherine Tucker
civilstoneware.com
Minimalist tableware inspired in part by Alabama waterways and the land surrounding them.

CREATIVE CENTER
Lowe Mill
lowemill.art
Former factory with 152 studios, seven galleries, plus performance spaces, community garden.

ZERO-WASTE
Natalie Chanin
alabamachanin.com
Sustainable fashion of Alabama Chanin and idea exchange at The School of Making.

INTERTWANGLEISM
Butch Anthony
museumofwonder.com
Drive-thru Museum of Wonder, with curiosities and Anthony's sought-after folk art.

LAYERED MEDIA
Doug Baulos
dougbaulos.com
Installations, paper collages, book pieces reflecting notions of mortality, memory and loss.

REGIONAL HUB
Black Belt Treasures Cultural Arts Center
blackbelttreasures.com
Repping more than 450 artists: painters, potters, sculptors and woodworkers.

EVENTS

BIRD-WATCHING

Alabama Coastal Birdfest

Gulf Coast, October

Walks and boat rides for peeping the hundreds of species that fly through during migration.

BLUES ROOTS

W.C. Handy Music Festival

Florence, July

Week of shows honoring Florence-born Handy as "Father of the Blues."

FOOTBALL

Iron Bowl

Tuscaloosa | Auburn November

Showdown between state's two big pigskin rivals: Alabama vs. Auburn.

ALABAMA ART

Kentuck Festival of the Arts

Northport, October

Exhibition for folk artists since 1953.

LOCAL AGRICULTURE

National Peanut Festival

Dothan, November

Harvest party, Peanut Capital of the World. George Washington Carver gave inaugural speech in 1938.

POWWOW

Moundville Native American Festival

Moundville, October

Education, celebration through art, dance, at ancient Indigenous site.

STATE HISTORY

CoalFest

Brilliant, May

Town named for coal quality celebrates bygone industry with live music, craft.

CRUSTACEAN CARNIVAL

National Shrimp Festival

Gulf Shores, October

Stroll boardwalk in long-running fete [50 years] for Gulf shrimp.

THEATER

Alabama Shakespeare Festival

Montgomery, July

One of the world's 10 largest Shakespeare fests. 400+ performances. Since 1972.

COASTAL PARTY

Hangout Music Festival

Gulf Shores, May

National acts [Stevie Wonder, Paul Simon, Tom Petty] play on beach between Gulf Shores and the sea.

REMEMBRANCE

Spirit of Our Ancestors Festival

Africatown, February

Clotilda Descendants Association gathers folks for stories of last known slave ship.

GRASSROOTS

Birmingham Folk Festival

Birmingham, May

Diverse expression, community vibes.

EXPERTS

MUSIC HISTORY
Terrell Benton
muscleshoalssoundstudio.org
Music industry pro, tour guide at Muscle Shoals Sound Studio. Encyclopedia of the tunes around here.

DOCUMENTARIAN
Annemarie Anderson
arts.alabama.gov
Oral historian, director of Alabama Center for Traditional Culture in Montgomery.

CONSERVATIONIST
Mitch Reid
nature.org
Working for forests, rivers, coasts in one of most biodiverse states in country.

SHEEP FARMING
Ana & Greg Kelly
dayspringdairy.com
First sheep-dairy in the state, Dayspring Dairy. Making cheeses, bourbon caramel.

ACTIVIST
Anthony Ray Hinton
eji.org
Public speaker, author. Spent 28 years on death row, wrongfully accused of killing two people.

MARINE SCIENCE
Cassie Bates
mobilebaykeeper.org
Scientist at Mobile Baykeeper working on measurable improvement to health of Coastal Alabama.

COMMENTARY
John Archibald
al.com/staff/jaarchib
Author, columnist, two-time winner of Pulitzer [2018, 2023 with son Ramsey].

COMMUNITY EVENTS
Soapy Jones
brasstackevents.com
Connecting community with jazz, burlesque, soap [Left Hand Soap Co.].

FOOD JUSTICE
Amanda Storey
jvtf.org
Community food access, youth education on food, farming, as executive director of Jones Valley Teaching Farm.

FOLKLORE
Dr. Kern Jackson
southalabama.edu
Professor, co-writer/producer of *Descendant*, doc on *Clotilda* ship.

RECIPE STORYTELLING
Lisa Cericola
southernliving.com
An editor at *Southern Living* shepherding stories of culture through food in a diverse South.

INNOVATION
Dr. Michael Curry
tuskegee.edu
Professor and founder/CEO of Eco-Friendly Plastic Materials.

CITIES & TOWNS

A guide to Alabama's college towns, music-making hamlets, history-filled hubs and bustling cities on the rise.

BIRMINGHAM

Birmingham's buttoned-up facade belies a liberated energy surging underneath. Led by native son Randall Woodfin, elected mayor at 36 years old in 2017, the city has been reinvigorated by younger generations. While communities like Mountain Brook and Homewood bring their own energy, we zero in more central. Start at beloved barista Jimmy Truong's JUNE COFFEE; bop next door to LAST CALL BAKING. A shopping quest reveals vintage treasure chest MK QUINLAN, brainchild of a style editor returned home, followed by next-door duo SHOPPE [garden supply] and GENERAL [home shop/cafe]. After pies at PIZZA GRACE, a nightcap fork in the road: romantic GOLDEN AGE WINE? Or tallboys at MOM'S BASEMENT? No wrong answers.

FARMERS MARKET	
Birdsong	POPULATION: 1,115,289
Check out Cericola Granola, Belle Meadow	COFFEE: Domestique
	BEST DAY OF THE YEAR: Sidewalk Film Festival, August

FLORENCE

Bucolic but bustling, Florence sits over the Tennessee River, called "Singing River" by the Yuchi people. Songs do famously pour from this corner, and musicians who call it home intersect with designers, chefs, painters and craftspeople. The morning gang gathers at ALL THE BEST, a vinyl shop/cafe inspired by Southern and Japanese convenience stores, from husbund-and-wife owners Kristy Bevis and record producer Ben Tanner. Peruse BILLY REID's flagship boutique; Florence's other fashion maven, Natalie Chanin, stocks her pieces a quick drive north. ODETTE is a standby for fare sourced from the likes of KODACHROME GARDENS. After dinner, locals perch on the rooftop of the GUNRUNNER HOTEL, sipping bourbon, talking big dreams.

SWIMMING HOLE	
Little Cypress Creek	POPULATION: 41,690
Hidden hangout along a crystal creek; enter at Wildwood Park	COFFEE: Rivertown
	BEST DAY OF THE YEAR: ShoalsFest, October

MONTGOMERY

Few streets hold as much history as Dexter Avenue [Rosa Parks boarded the bus at Court Square near Dexter Avenue Baptist Church, where Martin Luther King Jr. pastored], but there's a new energy here too. Trilogy Hotel gets its name from the rehab of three historic buildings. After drinks on its rooftop, dinner presents a choice of Italian or French: RAVELLO for Gulf snapper and gnocchi or FRENCHIE'S for moules frites. For outdoor action, MONTGOMERY WHITEWATER, a $90 million project, brings an Olympic-standard whitewater channel to town. And of course no visit is complete without the EQUAL JUSTICE INITIATIVE's National Memorial for Justice and Peace, a brutal, beautiful tribute to Black lynching victims.

HAPPY-HOUR SHOP	
Leroy Lounge	POPULATION: 198,986
Cosmopolitan cocktail bar and community watering hole	COFFEE: Prevail
	BEST DAY OF THE YEAR: Alabama Shakespeare Festival, spring

MOBILE

Alabama's only saltwater port sits atop of the bay that shares its name. Founded as capital of French Louisiana in 1702, it changed hands to the British, the Spanish and, finally, the Americans. This long history flows through architecture and cultural atmosphere in a fashion reminiscent of coastal cousin New Orleans. Caffeinate at Nova Espresso, then drop into THE MOBILE MUSEUM OF ART's extensive collection and exhibits, such as photographer Gordon Parks' *Segregation Story*, which documents 1950s life in rich color. Wander downtown to BRAIDED RIVER BREWING COMPANY, then through the live oaks of Oakleigh Garden Historic District. Join locals at The Hummingbird Way or CALLAGHAN'S IRISH SOCIAL CLUB, a local pillar noted for live music.

WATERING HOLE	
Hayley's Bar	POPULATION: 183,289
The dive-bar heart of Downtown Mobile	COFFEE: Serda's
	BEST DAY OF THE YEAR: Joe Cain Day, carnival season

HUNTSVILLE

Revolutionary War veteran John Hunt lent his name to what is now Alabama's largest city, when he settled around Big Spring in 1805. But the town's nickname, "The Rocket City," cemented its reputation. Even if you missed Space Camp as a kid, it's not too late to explore the United States Space and Rocket Center's exhibits. Other forms of science thrive here too: get to know the fast-growing brew scene with a double dip at **YELLOWHAMMER BREWING** and **STRAIGHT TO ALE**, close neighbors at Campus No. 805. Lowe Mill Arts & Entertainment, a massive onetime cotton mill, now houses artists' studios and shops, including the excellent **VERTICAL HOUSE RECORDS**. Catch a show at **ORION AMPHITHEATER** after dinner at local favorite **VIET HUONG**.

OUTDOOR SPOT

Monte Sano
Attention: mountain bikers, trail runners and hikers

POPULATION: 216,933

COFFEE: Gold Sprint

BEST DAY OF THE YEAR: PorchFest, May

TUSCALOOSA

Sitting on a fall line denoted by its major river, the Black Warrior, Tuscaloosa's northern half is Appalachian highlands: forested hills and cliffs that morph into the flat, open country of the Gulf Coastal Plain as you move south. Chief Tuskaloosa, a Mississippian leader who died at the hand of Hernando de Soto's expedition, is the namesake of town and waterway. Modern names like Bear Bryant and Nick Saban are ubiquitous now. If Bryant-Denny Stadium's 100,000-plus seats aren't an option, get your fix at **BRYANT MUSEUM**. Wade into an eternal barbecue debate by sampling ribs at **ARCHIBALD'S** or the original **DREAMLAND** at Jerusalem Heights. End your day at **DRUID CITY BREWING COMPANY** with an award-winning Downtown North Porter.

BREAKFAST STOP

City Cafe
Classic Northport spot for breakfast, meat-and-three

POPULATION: 100,602

COFFEE: Monarch Espresso

BEST DAY OF THE YEAR: The morning after the national championship, many Januaries

AUBURN

A university town that holds history and nostalgia, but it's ever-evolving too. Past the clock tower at Samford Hall, sits the shiny Tony and Libba Rane Culinary Science Center where students hone their skills in glass-front kitchens. Book a visit to the student-run rooftop and tasting-menu teaching restaurant **1865**. Or head out to Auburn's cool cousins — Opelika and Waverly. Stop by **SIDE TRACK**, a pay-what-you-want coffee shop, before perusing the sick stacks at 10,000 Hz Records. Destination distillery **JOHN EMERALD DISTILLING COMPANY** cooks up spirits for a cocktail. For dinner, it's smoked chicken and white sauce at **THE WAVERLY LOCAL** followed by **STANDARD DELUXE**, a musical portal and print shop that always brings pure magic.

INSTITUTION

Byron's Smokehouse
Barbecue favorite in an old Dairy Queen

POPULATION: 80,006

COFFEE: Auburn Oil Co. Booksellers

BEST DAY OF THE YEAR:
Old 280 Boogie, front porch fest

FAIRHOPE

Downtown bookstore **PAGE & PALETTE**, a golden-tiled mainstay, gives the first clue about this bayside town's nature. Long a laid-back haven for the creative—Fannie Flagg, Rick Bragg, Upton Sinclair, Winston Groom, et al.—Fairhope earned followers with its polished patina, moss-veiled oaks and gathering places. American Legion Post 199 hosts sunset concerts at the Tiki Bar stage, while **MANCI'S ANTIQUE CLUB**, a 1924 filling station turned dive bar in neighboring Daphne, is your Bloody Mary destination. **THE GRAND HOTEL** remains a resplendent [and updated] relic of Southern hospitality. **PROVISION**, a new multihyphenate market-bookstore-cafe weaves seamlessly into the vintage vibe, or pivot to a classic: oysters on the dock at **BLUEGILL**.

CAMPING

Lower Bartram Canoe Trail
Paddle to sleek, serene Mudhole Creek Shelter

POPULATION: 23,859

COFFEE: Kind Cafe

BEST DAY OF THE YEAR:
Arts & Crafts Festival, March

GULF SHORES / ORANGE BEACH

TRAIL

HUGH S. BRANYON BACKCOUNTRY

The beaches and towering condominiums of Gulf Shores and Orange Beach are beloved by spring breakers and family vacationers alike. Also here, a nuanced take on Gulf seafood at FISHER'S UPSTAIRS. The expansion along this waterfront is interrupted by GULF STATE PARK, a series of nature trails, an Angler's Academy, birdwatching, campground and THE LODGE, a newly refurbished [2018] Hilton project with a focus on sustainability.

DOTHAN

GO NUTS

SHUTE PECAN COMPANY

Situated southeast in the Wiregrass region, so named for the texture of its native grass, is the Peanut Capital of the World. Study the legacy of Dr. George Washington Carver [who developed more than 300 uses for the local peanut crop] at the GEORGE WASHINGTON CARVER INTERPRETIVE MUSEUM. Bird-watch at the DOTHAN AREA BOTANICAL GARDEN. Wiregrass Museum of Art and the city's mural project contribute to culture.

ANNISTON / GADSDEN

STATE'S HIGHEST POINT

CHEAHA STATE PARK

The FREEDOM RIDERS NATIONAL MONUMENT in Anniston includes the former Greyhound station where members of the Ku Klux Klan attacked civil rights activists in 1961. Before heading out of town, nourish the body with fried catfish at BETTY'S BAR-B-Q. In Gadsden, about 40 miles north along the Coosa River, the outdoors calls: hiking at Noccalula Falls Park, fly-fishing in Black Creek, or bouldering at Horse Pens 40, Hospital Boulders or Cherokee Rock Village.

MONROEVILLE

LITERARY TOWN CENTER

MONROE COUNTY MUSEUM

In the Literary Capital of Alabama, walk the sculpture trail showcasing 10 local writers, including the town's three Pulitzer winners: Harper Lee, Hank Williams and Cynthia Tucker [interview on page 89]. Time a visit with the annual performance of Lee's *To Kill a Mockingbird* and tour the Old Couthouse Museum. Burgers, fried chicken and Coke floats at MEL'S DAIRY DREAM, located on the site of Lee's childhood home.

ROAD TRIP

Take a journey through Alabama's rich history, artist enclaves, immigrant-inspired restaurants and natural wonders.

DAY 1

GREEK AND THREES IN BIRMINGHAM

Central Alabama's long-simmering stew of cultures, resources and labor changed the flavors of the foundational Southern meal.

Both self-explanatory and tantalizingly mysterious, the term "meat and three" shows up across the South. But in Birmingham, this plate lunch tells a specific story of the city's people. Basically, it comprises a plate [or styrofoam clamshell] bearing a protein and three vegetables—the latter, with poetic license. While more recognizable country-cooking and soul-food variations abound throughout the metro area [Eagle's Restaurant, a must], Birmingham distinctly claims the "Greek and three." When Greek immigrants and descendants started restaurants here, these innovators embraced time-honored Southern sides like mac and cheese and collard greens alongside saucy keftedes [meatballs] and pastitsio [baked pasta]. Four keepers of the flame:

THE BRIGHT STAR Just outside city limits in the industrial suburb of Bessemer, this portal to another time has been serving fish, steaks and mile-high pies since 1907. For lunch, order the fried red snapper throats swathed in lemon-butter sauce with Greek potatoes and shredded cabbage, then behold the singular glory of pineapple-cheese pie.

NIKI'S WEST The cafeteria-style steam table stretches into infinity. Items of note: lemon-pepper catfish, lamb with mint jelly, turnip greens. The stacked dessert case prompts further dilemmas.

JOHNNY'S Don't let the line deter you, or the very-not-historic strip-mall location. Timothy Hontzas' daily circus serves his family's recipes with fresher techniques and farm-sourced ingredients. Chicken thighs in a haunting honey-chipotle-coriander drizzle; charbroiled souvlaki in a near-nuclear garlicky lemon-tahini sauce; or fried Bayou La Batre shrimp with tangy, remoulade-esque "comeback sauce."

TED'S Passed down in 2000 from an established area Greek family to a more newly arrived one; Tasos and Beba Touloupis originally came to Alabama to study aerospace engineering and psychology, respectively. Their career pivot helped preserve a city institution, where they continue to serve Ted Sarris' Greek chicken and pastitsio. Pro protein moves: fried chicken livers, spaghetti and meat sauce or fried grouper.

FLOAT, FISH OR FLOWER-GAZE

Flow with one of the most biologically diverse rivers on the planet, the teeming Cahaba.

A 194-mile waterway running from Birmingham to Mobile Bay, the Cahaba is home to more native fish species than any other similarly sized river in the country—131 compared to, for example, the Colorado River watershed's 25.

FISH Fly-anglers frequent shady shallow spots like Pinchgut Creek and the Highway 280 dam. Bream and crappie are both common catches; redeye bass, more coveted. Follow expert Wes Frazer: *@touched.by.an.angler*.

FLOAT Lazy river the Cahaba is not. But with prep work, tubing proves mostly tranquil. Wear sturdy shorts and waterproof shoes to prevent below-deck scrapes. Limestone Park Canoe Rental for doughnuts to rent. 1531 *Limestone Pkwy, Brierfield*

FLORA Cahaba lilies, also known as swamp lilies, only grow in three states. Their petals last just 24 hours, so finding stands of these ivory fireworks feels extra magical. Launch a canoe or kayak at the Cahaba River National Wildlife Refuge, which also provides guided lily tours. 407 *Baby Bains Gap Rd, Anniston*

DAY 3

CIVIL RIGHTS SITES

Places to pay respect to the vital legacies of those who changed history, and to work toward healing.

MONTGOMERY With its interactive, artistically rendered and moving exhibits, it could take an entire day to experience the extraordinary programming at THE LEGACY MUSEUM and THE NATIONAL MEMORIAL FOR PEACE AND JUSTICE. If you see just one place in Alabama, this should be it.

For lunch, PANNIE-GEORGE'S serves soul food from a steam table inside the museum. Or head to BRENDA'S BAR-B-QUE PIT [since 1942], which nourished civil rights organizers, provided meeting space and disseminated event flyers. [For more sites, see the Montgomery city guide on page 28.]

SELMA Take U.S. 80 and you'll be traveling the 54-mile path [in reverse] voting rights activists took in 1965. At mile marker 80, stop by the LOWNDES COUNTY INTERPRETIVE CENTER, on the former site of Tent City, where tenant farmers and sharecroppers set up temporary homes after eviction for supporting the Voting Rights Act. In Selma, walk the iconic Edmund Pettus Bridge; on either end, you'll find NATIONAL VOTING RIGHTS MUSEUM AND INSTITUTE and Selma Interpretive Center, with the Ancient Africa, Enslavement, and Civil War Museum just down Water Street. The Martin Luther King Jr. Street Historic Walking Tour leads to BROWN CHAPEL AME CHURCH, where the Bloody Sunday march began after a communion service.

MARION Continue to Marion, about 30 miles northwest, where a state trooper shot activist Jimmy Lee Jackson in 1965, helping spark the Selma-to-Montgomery marches. [The trooper would not be sentenced until 2010.] Marion's legacy is not all tragedy: Corretta Scott King hails from this Black Belt town; she's recognized with others on the CIVIL RIGHTS FREEDOM WALL.

BIRMINGHAM Travel on to Birmingham to reflect at 16th Street Baptist Church. Across the street, the BIRMINGHAM CIVIL RIGHTS INSTITUTE is a place to hear Martin Luther King Jr.'s "Letter from a Birmingham Jail." KELLY INGRAM PARK served as a demonstration staging site. Close out a day at MICHAEL'S RESTAURANT inside the Negro Southern League Museum.

Additional sites in Tuskegee, pages 60; Anniston, p. 31; Monroeville, p.31.

DAY 4

THE COAST

A road (and ferry) romp along Alabama's 100 miles of shoreline.

MOBILE TO DAUPHIN ISLAND

Head south on Highway 193 to Dauphin Island. Admire fishing boats from 3-mile-long Gordon Persons Bridge. Where the highway tees at Bienville Boulevard, make a call. Westward, the road narrows past stilt-perched houses to West End Public Beach. The island keeps going for another 9 miles, and it's open for exploring by foot or boat, but it's remote. Head east for action: Fort Gaines, Dauphin Island Sea Lab, Audubon Bird Sanctuary. Mobile Bay Ferry heads for Fort Morgan. From there, continue on for the white sands of Gulf Shores and Orange Beach

ORANGE BEACH TO PERDIDO KEY

Perdido Pass slices through the shoreline, connecting the marinas of the Intercostal Waterway to the Gulf. While the pass would be the logical place for a state line, Florida and Alabama don't meet for another 2 miles. They do so with a flourish at the much-celebrated Flora-Bama. The original wood-framed watering hole was built in 1964 and has evolved into a labyrinthian palace of multiple stages, beach accesses and frosty Bushwackers galore.

BISCUITS, BIRDS AND BLUE HANDS IN THE BLACK BELT

A secluded, sylvan patch of Central Alabama holds both painful history and progressive movement.

Named for its rich raven soil and its Black-majority population, many descendants of enslaved cotton workers and, later, sharecroppers, Alabama's bucolic Black Belt recalls Upstate New York with its small farms, roads winding through meadows, and produce stands that lead into historic town squares. In a shade-dappled clearing off State Route 14 sits Heard Cemetery, final resting place of Jimmie Lee Jackson, whose murder by police in 1965 sparked the march from Selma to Montgomery. Jackson's gravestone—bullet-pocked and flower-crowned—provides a key to understanding both sides of the Black Belt: its pangs of the past and its people pushing forward. For an example of the latter, meet third-generation farmer CHRIS JOE, who welcomes birdwatchers seeking hawks, kites and songbirds on his family's Angus cattle farm with their CONNECTING WITH BIRDS AND NATURE TOURS. Projects by Auburn University's RURAL STUDIO dot downtown Newbern, from the firehouse to the library, all designed and built by students focused on rural living. Their $20K homes, part of the FRONT PORCH INITIATIVE's efforts to build affordable housing, have been shown at New York's MoMA and earned the program a Cooper Hewitt National Design Award. A few miles away, in Marion, chef SCOTT PEACOCK stands in a sun-streaked kitchen. The James Beard winner and co-author with Southern-cooking legend Edna Lewis now hosts waitlist-worthy biscuit-making "experiences" at historic mansion Reverie. Over in Greensboro, textile artist AARON SANDERS HEAD grows cosmos and indigo, in a dye garden outside his home, with his partner, musician Tim Higgins. Students leave his natural-dyeing workshops with cerulean-stained hands plus pillows, quilts and handkerchiefs in brilliant blues, oranges and coppers.

SOUTH BY NORTH AFRICA

Daughter of an Egyptian mother and Alabama-born father, baker Sarah Cole is set to open ABADIR'S *in a permanent location in Greensboro. Until then, Cole pops up around town with freshened familiars: coconut yogurt cake, tahini orange rolls and shortbread cookies filled with dates.*

SELECTED CONTENT

MORE THAN 25 ENTRIES

Excerpts have been edited for clarity and concision.

A deep dive into the cultural heritage of Alabama through news clippings, timelines, writings and other historical hearsay

STARS FELL ON ALABAMA

Carl Cramer, 1934

Alabama felt a magic descending, spreading, long ago. Since then it has been a land with a spell on it—not a good spell, always. Moons, red with the dust of barren hills, thin pine trunks barring horizons, festering swamps, restless yellow rivers, are all part of a feeling—a strange certainty that above and around them hovers enchantment—an emanation of malevolence that threatens to destroy men through dark ways of its own. It is difficult to translate this feeling into words, yet almost every visitor to this land has known it and felt in some degree what I felt with increasing wonder during the six years I lived there. The stranger is more apt to realize that sorcery is at work on these people and know that the land on which they live is its apprentice. What the strange influence is or when it began is a matter for debate. It is a legend that the great chief Tush-ka-lusa, upon the accidental death of his son at the hands of one of De Soto's men, drew himself up to his seven-foot height and, standing over his dead boy's body, called down upon all white invaders of this land the vengeance of the Great Spirit. And it is pointed out as one of many proofs of the power of his curse that from that day to this no year has passed in which the Black Warrior River has not claimed at least one victim. Others say that the enchantment began in the year that [women] in a Cherokee tribe, whose tepees were pitched near what is now the town of Oxford, Alabama, bore on the same day sons that were spotted as the leopard. The mothers were tried for witchcraft and sentenced to be burned—but when the flames licked about their bound feet the earth yawned and took them and all the tribe into itself. They lie now beneath the bottomless pit that is filled by the clear waters of Blue Pond. So the witch-mothers triumphed and they still rule Alabama. But those who really know, the black conjure women in their weathered cabins along the Tombigbee, tell a different story. They say that on the memories of the oldest slaves their fathers knew there was one indelible imprint of an awful event—a shower of stars over Alabama. Many an Alabamian to this day reckons dates from "the year the stars fell"—though he and his neighbor frequently disagree as to what year of our Lord may be so designated. All are sure, however, that once upon a time stars fell on Alabama, changing the land's destiny. What has been written in eternal symbols was thus erased—and the region has existed ever since, unreal and fated, bound by a horoscope such as controls no other country.

JAZZ STANDARD

"We lived our little drama.
We kissed in a field of white
And stars fell on Alabama last night."

The tune "Stars Fell on Alabama" takes its inspiration from the 1934 *Carl Cramer book of the same name, about the dramatic Leonid meteor shower in Alabama in November* 1833. *Composed by Frank Perkins with lyrics by Mitchell Parish, the song has been recorded by more than* 100 *artists, including the following:*

Guy Lombardo and His Royal Canadians 1934
Richard Himber and His Ritz-Carlton Orchestra, vocals by Joey Nash 1934
Kay Starr 1948
The Stan Getz Quintet 1953
Art Tatum, Lionel Hampton and Buddy Rich 1955
Ella Fitzgerald and Louis Armstrong 1956
Anita O'Day 1956
Frankie Laine and Buck Clayton 1956
Billie Holiday 1957
Doris Day 1957
Frank Sinatra 1957
The Sonny Stitt Quartet 1958
Cannonball Adderley and John Coltrane 1959
Ricky Nelson 1961
Bing Crosby 1975
Jimmy Buffett 1980
Harry Connick Jr 1988
Sun Ra 1990
Tara Nevins 2011
She & Him 2014
Lizz Wright 2017
Taylor Hicks 2021

The Jacksonville State University Marching Band in Jacksonville, Alabama, a long-time incubator for band educators nationwide, also performs a stirring arrangement of "Stars Fell on Alabama" at every home game, with the band's more than 500 *members spanning the entire length of the field.*

THE CLOTILDA

The year was 1859—about 52 years after the supposed end to the transatlantic slave trade—but Timothy Meaher figured he could get away with it. The wealthy shipyard owner had a schooner built called *Clotilda* that would carry 110 African men, women and children away from their homes and into slavery at Mobile Bay. The ship's captain, William Foster, ordered it burned and sunk. It would take 160 more years to find it.

Meanwhile, following the end of the Civil War, *Clotilda*'s survivors formed the Africatown community and stewarded their heritage despite challenges. In 2019, when the discovery of the *Clotilda* was confirmed, Slave Works Project co-director, Paul Gardullo, told *Smithsonian* magazine: "This was a search not only for a ship. This was a search to find our history and this was a search for identity, and this was a search for justice."

YELLOW HAMMER

When the clock expires on a University of Alabama football victory, the Million Dollar Band strikes up for the faithful in a strutting hymn of ecstasy, pride, relief—or all three, depending on the game. An Iron Bowl rendition would sound like this:

Hey, Auburn!
Hey, Auburn!
We just beat the hell out of you
Rammer Jammer, Yellow Hammer
Give 'em hell, Alabama!

The yellowhammer is Alabama's state bird [see page 44], but in Tuscaloosa, it's also the name of a potent cocktail that's been served at Gallettes since 1976. The recipe is, of course, a closely guarded secret. You can find solid guesses online: there's rum, there's citrus, possibly amaretto, maybe vodka. But as with all home imitations, it's nearly impossible to match the concoction—doled out in the bright yellow souvenir cups that are ubiquitous in Tuscaloosa—and its environment. Gallettes sits on the end of the Strip, a stone's throw from Bryant-Denny Stadium, and on a game day weekend they'll pour thousands of gallons of Yellow Hammers, weaving the drink into the lore that is Alabama football.

MOBILE MARDI GRAS

Every year on the Sunday before Fat Tuesday, revelers in Mobile gather at Church Street Graveyard to witness Cain's Merry Widows, a women's mystic society founded in 1974, as they lay a wreath on a gravestone while dressed and veiled entirely in black. The inscription:

HERE LIES OLD JOE CAIN
THE HEART AND SOUL OF MARDI GRAS IN MOBILE
In 1866, Joe Cain dressed as a mythical Chickasaw chief, and might have seemed comic—but certain perceptive ones realized he represented the epitome of victory—for the Chickasaws were never defeated in all their history. So Joe Cain, with his masquerade, lifted this region from despair and revived the ancient French observance of Boeuf Gras—now known in Mobile as Mardi Gras.

Mobile's celebratory tradition dates back to 1703, when the newly founded town was the capital of French Louisiana; Mobilians are not shy in pointing out that this makes it America's oldest Mardi Gras. Locals take time in their revelry to recognize Joe Cain, the controversial man and former Confederate soldier who led a one-wagon parade in the days of Reconstruction and revamped Carnival season for Alabama's port city.

Learn more on Mobile's Mardi Gras—including its history of segregation—in the 2008 year documentary The Order of Myths.

SACRED HARP

Daily Mountain Eagle, *Jasper, Alabama, March 14, 1923*
"There will be an all day singing in the Sacred Harp book at Mt. Vernon the second Sunday in April. Everybody invited, especially good singers."

Sacred Harp, an ongoing folk tradition of singing choral music a capella, originated with a shape note tunebook, *The Sacred Harp*, published in 1844. T Bone Burnett recorded Sacred Harp at Liberty Baptist Church in Henagar for the soundtrack of 2003 film *Cold Mountain*. A 2006 documentary, *Awake, My Soul,* follows the tradition. Sacred Harp Musical Heritage Association is based in Huntsville, holds annual Camp Fasola.

BIRDS OF NOTE

GOLDEN EAGLE *Aquila chrysaetos* Large, long-winged and well-armed with beak and talons, the golden eagle boasts gleaming neck feathers, flaunted while soaring. Alabama has a strong wintering population.

SANDHILL CRANE *Antigone canadensis* That rich, trumpeting call? It's likely a sandhill crane. Other tell-tale signs: crimson-capped heads and exuberant dance skills come courting time.

BAY-BREASTED WARBLER *Setophaga castanea* Voracious predators of spruce budworms, these songbirds transform from season to season: summer hues of cream, umber and gray shift to autumn greens and whites.

NORTHERN FLICKER *Colaptes auratus* Alabama's state bird is also known as the yellowhammer. Of the woodpecker family but, unlike most other woodpeckers, migratory.

LONG-EARED OWL *Asio otus* Secretive, nocturnal. Jaunty ear tufts lend a distinct expression of surprise, but also super-sharp hearing for tracking prey in total darkness.

BELTED KINGFISHER *Megaceryle alcyon* Trollers of rivers, streams and shorelines. Males have one blue band across a white breast, while females sport a blue and a chestnut band; both have hefty bills for fishing.

AMERICAN KESTREL *Falco sparverius* The smallest falcon of all still packs a punch with its *killy-killy-killy* call and fierce aerial dives. Awash in color, from gray-blue to rust and red. Any farmland drive could yield a sighting.

RUBY-THROATED HUMMINGBIRD *Archilochus colubris* Brilliant lightning flashes of jewel green and red, moving at 53 wingbeats a minute. They seek nectar along woodland edges and in densely flowering places like gardens.

Among many prime spots statewide—from **GUNTERSVILLE STATE PARK** *to the Coastal Birding Trail—the Black Belt is home to* **THE JOE FARM**. *Christopher Joe and his family noticed birdlife teeming around their farmland and allied with Alabama Audubon to host birders from all over the country as part of the* **BLACK BELT BIRDING FESTIVAL**.

RURAL STUDIO

At the acclaimed Auburn University design-build program Rural Studio, students pursue social change through thoughtful architecture and design. Projects address issues of home access and affordability, small-scale farming, energy efficiency and more. To date, there have been more than 200 *projects—and more than* 1,200 *participating students—in the Black Belt. Below, selected regional creations.*

PERRY LAKES COVERED BRIDGE

Marion

Steel, wood and salvaged tin improve park navigation.

AKRON BOYS AND GIRLS CLUB

Akron

Swooping, barrel-like lamella structure shelters basketball court.

HORSESHOE COURTYARD

Greensboro

Gritty, unloved outdoor space becomes a nonprofit's stately courtyard.

NEWBERN TOWN HALL

Newbern

Blocks of cypress and steel framing make for striking civic architecture.

HARRIS/BUTTERFLY HOUSE

Masons Bend

Angular roofline, covered porch.

SMOKE HOUSE

Mason's Bend

A fisherman's smokehouse fashioned from cast-off concrete and old road signs.

MUSIC MAN HOUSE

Greensboro

Eccentric collage of materials matches owner's sensibility.

THINNINGS TEA HOUSE

Payne Lake

Experimental use of skinny invasive trees, usually discarded.

FAUNSDALE COMMUNITY CENTER

Faunsdale

New structure inserted into old city hall's brick shell.

LIONS PARK SCOUT HUT

Greensboro

Small, stacked timbers bolster angled walls.

ROSE LEE'S HOUSE

Newbern

"Expandable" home inspired by local farmhouse structures.

HERO PLAYGROUND

Greensboro

Simple, slatted structures and repurposed telephone poles become a kids' dream park.

OPERATION PAPERCLIP

"My brother invented the V-2. We want to surrender." With these words, two brothers on bicycles gave themselves up to American forces in May 1945. So how did Nazi Party member 5,738,692, Wernher von Braun, world's foremost rocket expert, go from developing missiles for Hitler to propelling Americans into space from Huntsville, Alabama? Operation Paperclip.

Von Braun and his brother Magnus spent the final days of the war fleeing the SS after Hitler ordered all "technical men" associated with rocketry development to be liquidated. Moving west toward the Allies rather than risk capture by the Soviets, their surrender to the Americans was by design, and expedient for all involved: "We knew that we had created a new means of warfare, and the question as to what nation, to what victorious nation we were willing to entrust this brainchild of ours was a moral decision more than anything else." The Allied intelligence community had von Braun at the top of their Black List, a compendium of the Reich's top scientific minds wanted for interrogation. [At war's end, 1,600 German scientists were resettled in the States.] By September 1945, von Braun and his staff found themselves in America, with orders to continue their experiments and research in rocketry. The moral cost of this transaction is not exactly calcuable. Under Hitler, von Braun's V-2 had been manufactured by slave labor, and more than 20,000 concentration camp prisoners died building it—which von Braun acknowledged knowing, but feeling powerless to change. He was relocated to Huntsville in 1950, where he developed the Redstone rocket, the United States' first nuclear ballistic missile, a direct descendent of the V-2. Atop a Redstone rocket, Alan Shepard became the first American in space in 1961.

ALABAMA BLUES PROJECT

W.C. Handy of Florence published "Memphis Blues" in 1921, considered the first blues song. These days, Alabama Blues Project surely does him proud. Since 1995, the nonprofit has provided Blues education and music lessons to students ages six to 18 to preserve the heritage of the art form in both traditional and contemporary ways. The project includes Blues in Schools curriculum, After-School Blues Clubs and Blues Camps with performances by local musicians. *alabamablues.org*

JUBILEE

Excitement Among the Fish
Mobile Daily Register, July 17, 1867

"Large numbers of crabs, flounders and other fish were found at the water's edge, and taken in out of the wet... They all appear to forsake the deep water, and swim and cluster in immense numbers to the shore."

The first known instance of a newspaper covering a "jubilee"—a phenomenon that happens only in Mobile Bay, Alabama, and Tokyo, Japan—happened in the mid-1800s. But its occurrence stretches back much further to a time unknown. Marine biologists believe a particular set of factors can lead to an accumulation of organic matter on the bay floor and cause a lack of oxygen. It sends fish to shore, gasping for air there, sometimes flinging themselves out of the water completely. Locals know to make the most of these moments, which occur most often in summer and pre-dawn, by scooping up what they can—shrimp, blue crab, flounder!

THE TALLADEGA CURSE

Constructed on a former air force base in 1969, Talladega Superspeedway is the longest NASCAR oval at 2,660 miles, with a crowd capacity of 175,000. The speedway is noted as the site of the fastest-ever speed achieved by a NASCAR vehicle on a closed-oval course: 216.309 miles per hour, by Rusty Wallce in 2004. Talladega is also home to an ominous legend. Numerous bizarre occurrences began as early as 1973. NASCAR Rookie of the Year Larry Smith died of a head injury in a mysterious solo crash. During the same race, driver Bobby Isaac parked his car and quit for the season because, he said, a voice told him to. The following year, 10 cars were mechanically sabotaged the night before the race, and several other deaths on and off the track at Talladega followed. While the origin story of the curse varies [explanations often devolve into familiar clichés about Indigenous curses, "burial grounds" and the like], what is certain is that the Alabama track retains an aura of the intimidating and unexpected.

RECORDED IN THE SHOALS

Cities that make up The Shoals in northwestern Alabama include Florence, Muscle Shoals, Tuscumbia, and Sheffield. The legendary FAME Studios is located in Muscle Shoals while Muscle Shoals Sound Studio is in Sheffield. A sampling of artists who recorded in the region:

Arthur Alexander
Duane Allman
Joan Baez
Band of Horses
The Black Keys
The Blind Boys of Alabama
Jimmy Buffett
J.J. Cale
Clarence Carter
Cher
Jimmy Cliff
Joe Cocker
Dire Straits
Bob Dylan
Aretha Franklin
Donnie Fritts
Glenn Frey
Simon & Garfunkel
Bobbie Gentry
R.B. Greaves
Levon Helm
Millie Jackson
Etta James
Elton John
Julian Lennon

Delbert McClinton
Willie Nelson
Cat Stevens
Wilson Pickett
John Prine
Bonnie Raitt
Lou Rawls
Otis Redding
Linda Ronstadt
The Rolling Stones
Leon Russell
Carlos Santana
Bob Seger
Paul Simon
Lynyrd Skynyrd
Boz Scaggs
Percy Sledge
St. Paul & the Broken Bones
The Staple Singers
Chris Stapleton
Candi Staton
Rod Stewart
Traffic
John Paul White
Bobby Womack

BARBECUE LEGENDS

Alabama barbecue comprises many styles, methods and sauces with influences from West Africa, Appalachia to Greece. Then of course there's the state's unique contribution to slathering praxis—Alabama white sauce. Here, some practitioners of the art who sweep the range.

ARCHIBALD'S 1211 *Martin Luther King Jr Blvd, Northport* George and Betty Archibald left jobs in the steel mill and paper mill, respectively, to open a barbecue restaurant in 1962. Still family run, still serving ribs and vinegar-based sauce.

BIG BOB GIBSON BAR-B-Q 1715 *6th Ave SE [U.S. 31] and 2520 Danville Rd SW, Decatur* Original home to Alabama white sauce [see origin story page 57]. The vinegar-mayo concoction enhances smoked poultry—fitting for North Alabama, where chicken farms abound.

BOB SYKES BAR-B-Q 1724 *9th Ave N, Bessemer* It began with a gamble when Maxine and Bob Sykes sold their house and car to open a restaurant in 1957. Serving pork shoulders, ribs and poultry.

DEMETRI'S BBQ 1901 *28th Ave S, Homewood* Part of the deep tradition of Greek immigrants in the Alabama restaurant business Demetri Nakos emigrated from Corfu to Birmingham in 1955 and learned barbecue from his uncle. Demetri's sauce recipe comes from his wife's aunt's husband, also Greek.

DREAMLAND BAR-B-QUE *original location at 5535 15th Ave E, Tuscaloosa* Look at the menu with indecision too long and a server is liable to deliver direction: "This is Dreamland, honey. We have ribs." Original menu: Full or half slabs with a stack of white bread on paper plate.

GOLDEN RULE BAR-B-Q AND GRILL 2504 *Crestwood Blvd, Irondale* Opened 1891, making it one of the oldest barbecue restaurants still in operation. Sauces span styles—mustard to sweeter versions.

LANNIE'S BAR-B-Q SPOT 2115 *Minter Ave, Selma* Lannie and Will Travis opened their restaurant as a weekend operation in 1944. During rigid segregation of the 1960s, it offered a welcome table to Black and white patrons. Now with two locations.

ATHLETES OF NOTE

More than football, Alabama has been home to many greats across sport. A sampling:

HANK AARON *Mobile*
Broke Babe's long-standing homerun record

BO JACKSON *Bessemer*
Heisman winner, NFL and MLB All-Star

JENNIFER CHANDLER *Lincoln*
Gold medals [1975 Pan Am, Olympics] in diving

DAVEY ALLISON *Hueytown*
1987 NASCAR Rookie of the Year, 1992 driver of the year

CHARLES BARKLEY *Leeds*
Auburn alum, NBA All-Star and MVP

EVANDER HOLYFIELD *Atmore*
Undisputed boxing champion in two weight classes

MIA HAMM *Selma*
Two-time Olympic gold medalist in soccer

CARL LEWIS *Birmingham*
Nine Olympic gold medals in track and field

DONNA JEAN GODCHAUX

Cue up just about any version of "Playing in the Band" from 1972 to 1979, and there she is: Florence, Alabama's Donna Jean Godchaux, her voice soaring over the Grateful Dead as they drop into one of their famous improvisation sections. Donna Jean, along with her then-husband Keith, put her stamp on the Dead world, touring and recording with the band and its offshoots for nearly a decade. If the Dead wasn't touring, the Jerry Garcia Band was, and Donna was onstage beside him night after night, immortalized on tapes and archival releases. She's there on Jerry Garcia's *Reflections* and *Cats Under the Stars*, and on Bob Weir's *Ace*. But if you want to hear Donna before she carved out a place for herself in psychedelic-rock lore—and The Rock and Roll Hall of Fame—pull up Percy Sledge's "When a Man Loves a Woman" or Elvis Presley's "Suspicious Minds"—small samples of her work as a Muscle Shoals session singer.

HARVEY UPDYKE

The Iron Bowl, the annual meeting between the University of Alabama and Auburn University, simmers in the background of the state's daily life. On any given day, *The Paul Finebaum Show*, a radio staple of football culture in Alabama, testifies to the big game's primacy, with characters and plotlines that fall somewhere between Southern Gothic Shakespeare and professional wrestling. On January 27, 2011 "Al from Dadeville" dialed in to Finebaum's show and made the vitriol manifest. He announced on air that he had poisoned the 76-year-old landmark oak trees at Toomer's Corner, a gathering place for Auburn fans to mark victories and notable occasions by throwing toilet paper high into the trees' limbs. "They're not dead yet," he said, "but they definitely will die." The Auburn police called the show minutes later to investigate. "Al" turned out to be the nom de guerre of Harvey Updyke, a retired Texas state trooper and diehard Alabama fan. He was so incensed by the Tide's 2010 Iron Bowl loss that he had driven to Auburn the following weekend and dropped enough Spike 80DF herbicide around the living monuments to put the safety of the local water supply into question. After cutting down the beloved trees, workers had to remove the soil beneath Toomer's Corner to a depth of 8 feet. Auburn fans were outraged, while most Alabama fans moved quickly to distance themselves through fundraisers and public displays of condemnation. Updyke ultimately spent more than 70 days in prison and was ordered to pay $800,000 in damages, an amount he put but little dent in by his death in 2020. He spent his last days remorseful for his actions, likening it to a joke gone too far; Finebaum, for one, believed him. The trees were replaced and [following an act of vandalism] replaced again. Auburn's cherished tradition remains on pause.

CHITLIN' CIRCUIT

From the 1930s to late '60s, a collection of venues across the eastern half of the United States formed an oasis for Black performers and patrons, in what became known as the Chitlin' Circuit. It's estimated that West Montgomery alone had 19 clubs, including the prestigious Laicos Club [*social* spelled backward], played by B.B. King and other legends. The Carver Performing Arts Theatre in Birmingham holds some of the history. Opened in 1935 as a movie theater welcoming Black patrons, after a closure and renovations, it celebrated a grand reopening in 2022. It now hosts performances and is headquarters for the Alabama Jazz Hall of Fame.

INDIGENOUS HISTORY

The path Eastern Woodland peoples of Alabama, Georgia, Tennessee, North Carolina walked as they were forcibly expelled from their land—now known as the Trail of Tears—threads through the top of the state. These sites offer ways to learn about and commemorate Alabama's first peoples.

MANITOU CAVE An important spiritual center for Native Americans, with some of the first earliest known evidence of the Cherokee language etched on its limestone walls. *manitoucaveofal.org*

LAKE GUNTERSVILLE STATE PARK Two westward routes on the Trail, one by water, one land, now part of a state park on the Tennessee River. 1155 *Lodge Dr, Guntersville*

RHODES FERRY PARK Where 2,300 Cherokees became the only group displaced via rail. 100 *Market St NE, Decatur*

MOUNDVILLE ARCHAEOLOGICAL PARK The site of a major Mississippian city, circa 1000-1450 C.E., with more than two dozen mounds and hundreds of artifacts. *moundville.museums.ua.edu*

WICHAHPI STONE WALL Largest unmortared rock wall in the U.S., and largest memorial to a Native American woman. Built by Tom Hendrix for his great-great-grandmother, a Yuchi woman forced from the area who later returned by a five-year journey on foot. 13890 *Lauderdale County 8, Florence*

HISTORY MUSEUM OF MOBILE Exhibit details South Alabama tribes, including Bottle Creek's 18 mounds. *historymuseumofmobile.co*

The state of Alabama recognizes nine Indigenous nations: Echota Cherokee Tribe of Alabama, Cherokee Tribe of Northeast Alabama, Ma-Chis Lower Creek Indian Tribe of Alabama, Southeastern Mvskoke Nation, Cher-O-Creek Intra-Tribal Indians, MOWA Band of Choctaw Indians, Piqua Shawnee Tribe, United Cherokee AniYunWiYa Nation, and Poarch Band of Creek Indians, the only one of the nine also recognized by the federal government.
poarchcreekindians.org

BLESSING OF THE FLEET

Colorful pennant flags flap and flowers hang from the shrimp boats at the docks in Bayou La Batre each May. Townspeople gather for gumbo and Vietnamese cuisine as the archbishop offers a blessing, a hope for abundance and safety for the local fisherfolk. The gathering has been hosted by St. Margaret Parish since 1949, back when a simple boiled shrimp lunch was offered for about 50 cents.

After the fall of Saigon in 1975, two-thirds of Vietnam's professional fishers left, often arriving at Eglin Air Force Base on the Florida Panhandle. The experienced shrimpers, who come from generations of seagoing families, took quickly to work in the Gulf Coast's fishing and seafood-processing industries. Approximately one-third of Bayou La Batre's population today is of Asian descent, including Rev. Michael Long Vu at St. Margaret's. In recent years, natural disasters and seafood imports have caused hardships for the community. Organizations like Boat People SOS help provide resources and solidarity.

"TAKE A LETTER MARIA"

"Take a Letter Maria" by R.B. Greaves is not the most famous song to come out of Muscle Shoals, but for David Hood, Roger Hawkins, Barry Beckett and Jimmy Johnson, it might have been the most important. After racking up hits as session players at Rick Hall's FAME, they struck out on their own with Muscle Shoals Sound Studio. But for much of 1969, The Swampers were anxious small-business owners, sitting on Jackson Highway in a converted coffin showroom, waiting for the phone to ring. In late summer, it finally did. They cut "Take a Letter Maria" with Greaves on August 19, 1969. It peaked at #2 on the *Billboard* Hot 100 in September, and by November had been certified Gold. In December, The Rolling Stones arrived, spending three days at Jackson Highway and leaving with three songs: "You Gotta Move," "Brown Sugar" and "Wild Horses." The Muscle Shoals Rhythm Section kept the lights on and the doors open, and eventually made records with a stack of clients including the Staple Singers, Paul Simon, Lynyrd Skynyrd and Bob Dylan.

SUN RA

Born—officially—in Birmingham, 1914, *under the name Herman Pool Blount, the jazz visionary and extraplanetary icon Sun Ra became a key figure in* 1960s *musical innovation and the birth of the Afrofuturist movement in arts and letters.*

"MY MUSIC IS WORDS"

Some people are of this world, others are not. My natural self is not of this world because this world is not of my not and nothingness, alas and happily, at last I can say this world is this unfortunate planet. The destiny of this planet is at stake, one fatal further mistake can cause its long delayed destruction. One fatal mistake can be its last mistake. The future is obvious, but the potential impossible is calling softly and knocking gently ... calling softly to the natural selves of nothingness according to the standards of infinity nature and infinity nature's BEING ... knocking gently upon the door of those who are of nature and nature's God. There are other dimensions and the equation of it is every other world in the infinity of the universe. This is the why of the music I represent; and this is the why of the image of a better world: the alter-life for the alter-life is different from the life of this world. ... Nature ... intuition ... psychic harmonization ... NATURE ... INTUITION ... PSYCHIC HARMONIZATION! LIVING SYMBOLS OF DISCIPLINE ... happiness for and from the greater universe. —*Excerpted from* The Cricket, *issue* 1, 1968

As jazz swept up from New Orleans through the South, a host of Alabamians left their mark. **NAT "KING" COLE** *of Montgomery became a jazz to pop sensation.* **DINAH WASHINGTON** *hailed from Tuscaloosa, where the city's cultural arts center bears her name. Mobile-born trombonist* **URBIE GREEN** *played on her recordings as well as those of Billie Holiday and Sinatra, while Mobile-born trombonist* **FRED WESLEY** *dropped jazz influence into* **JAMES BROWN** *recordings and shows. Band leaders like* **JAMES REESE EUROPE** *and* **ERSKINE HAWKINS** *left indelible marks* [pages 69 and 70], *on American music.*

WHITE SAUCE

The distinctive barbecue tradition goes under the lens in this poem by Jason McCall.

WHEN MY WIFE GETS TO TELL YOU ABOUT WHITE SAUCE

She'll tell you everything
starts with the rivalry between

Whitt's and Big Bob Gibson.
She'll let you know that people who really know

white sauce know to order the turkey
and not the chicken. And she knows

how to tell who goes too heavy
on the mayonnaise and too light on the vinegar.

And these lessons don't matter because I love
white sauce because I actually hate white sauce,

but I love listening to my wife tell the world
how much she knows because after two strokes

there are times when she doesn't know the right way
to hold a knife or how to add

tax on a receipt. And every time I see her struggle I want
a minute in the octagon with whatever god

decided to crack her brain open twice.
But a minute boxing god is a minute I lose

of her talking someone through the right
amount of pepper or how much you can tell

just by watching the sauce drip from a fork.
And this is why we always need someone

like Prometheus stealing fire from heaven. Maybe
this is why someone needed to know it was possible

to look back on Sodom even if God turned the eyes
to salt first. Maybe we all need to know we can have something

the gods can't take away, even if it's just a memory
of what good barbecue sauce is supposed to taste like.

Jason McCall is the author of the essay collection Razed by TV Sets. *His other books include* What Shot Did You Ever Take *[co-written with Brian Oliu]*; A Man Ain't Nothin'; Two-Face God; Mother, Less Child *[co-winner of the 2013 Paper Nautilus Vella Chapbook Prize]*; Dear Hero, *[winner of the 2012 Marsh Hawk Press Poetry Prize and co-winner of the 2013 Etchings Press Whirling Prize]*; I Can Explain; *and* Silver. *He and P.J. Williams are the editors of* It Was Written: Poetry Inspired by Hip-Hop. *He is a native of Montgomery, Alabama currently teaches at the University of North Alabama.. This poem first appeared in issue* 86 *[winter 2023] of* Gravy *from the Southern Foodways Alliance.*

WHITE SAUCE ORIGINS

In 1925, a railroad worker known as Big Bob Gibson opened a barbecue restaurant in Decatur. His mayonnaise-based white barbecue sauce, along with a more traditional tomato-vinegar sauce, made the menu from day one. While the origin story is murky, pitmaster Chris Lilly, who is married to Big Bob's great-granddaughter, Amy, and keeps the Gibson family barbecue tradition running today, told *Alabama* writer Matt Wake that the fat in the mayo might have been used to preserve moisture in smoked poultry. "People describe it as a mayonnaise sauce," Lilly said, "but I would describe it as a vinegar sauce with mayonnaise in it, more than anything." Along with those two key ingredients, the sauce, as it exists today, typically contains various other additions [depending on the cook], such as lemon juice, Worcestershire, hot sauce, mustard or horseradish.

ALABAMA
AUBURN

IRON BOWL

1893 For their inaugural meeting, Alabama and Auburn play a February game. The Tigers come out on top, 32-22. But the teams immediately disagree on whether it's the final game of the season or the season opener. Rivalry ensues.

1964 In the first televised Iron Bowl, quarterback Joe Namath leads Alabama to victory, 21-14.

1972 Auburn trails undefeated Alabama by 13 points with just six minutes in the game. The Tigers block two punts, running both of them back for touchdowns—and a win, 17-16. The Tide's national championship chances are dashed.

1981 Alabama beats Auburn 28-17. Paul "Bear" Bryant breaks college football record with 315 wins.

1982 With 2:26 in the game — Auburn down by five points and nine straight Bama losses—Auburn freshman Bo Jackson sails a final yard over defenders into the end zone. Goal posts come down.

2013 "Kick Six": A last-second Alabama field goal falls short into Chris Davis's arms; 109 yards of delirium [and crushing blocks] later, Auburn wins the football game.

IRON INTERRUPTED

The Iron Bowl enjoys a reputation as one of the fiercest rivalries in college sports, but for a period of 41 years, from 1907 until 1948, Alabama and Auburn ceased to meet on the field. The cause? A contract dispute between the two schools over $34. In lieu of vying for football supremacy, the two institutions fought a proxy war over funding, political appointments and the placement of New Deal agencies, with battles in Montgomery becoming so heated that Auburn president Luther Duncan declared one Tuscaloosa-produced report on the state of higher education in Alabama to be "just like the doctrine of Hitler." Since the time that hostilities were returned to the football field, the game has featured such names as Bear Bryant, Shug Jordan, Joe Namath, Bo Jackson and, more recently, Nick Saban and Cam Newton. And after decades playing at Birmingham's Legion Field, it has since 2000 been played as a home-and-home series, with each school hosting the game at its campus stadium on alternate years.

TUSKEGEE UNIVERSITY IN THE NEWS

LEXINGTON HERALD LEADER

April 14, 1901

"Booker T. Washington, founder of the Tuskegee Institute For Colored Students is just now making his bow as an author. His autobiographical volume, 'Up From Slavery,' recently issued, is being highly praised by reviewers."

THE MONTGOMERY ADVERTISER

November 25, 1917

"It is well to get a glimpse of the work of a man who has spent years studying the uses and purposes of our soils and rocks, our trees and shrubbery, our wild plants and our cultivated field crops. This man is Prof. George W. Carver, the research scientist of Tuskegee Institute. Prof. Carver has given the greater part of his life to discovering and putting into useful form the purposes of the products of our soils.… There is nothing mystic or high-browish about either Prof. Carver or his work. Everything he has done or is doing is toward practical, useful, purposeful ends. Much that he has accomplished has already been useful in many kitchens and in many fields here in the Central South. He has helped folks, is helping them now and will continue to help them. His life is a life of service to the South."

THE TUSKEGEE HERALD

June 23, 1953

"Ralph Ellison, author of 'Invisible Man,' returned to Tuskegee Institute Monday after an absence of nearly 17 years. In this time he has developed into one of the nation's foremost novelists. For his book, 'Invisible Man,' he received the 1952 National Book Award's citation and gold plaque. The award was for the outstanding novel of the year."

THE NEW YORK TIMES

December 9, 2008

"When the Tuskegee Airmen, the all-black force of elite pilots, emerged from combat in World War II, they faced as much discrimination as they had before the war. It was not until six decades later that their valor was recognized and they received the Congressional Gold Medal, the highest civilian honor Congress can give."

HORSE PENS 40

Pull into the parking lot at Horse Pens 40 on a crisp winter morning and you're nearly as likely to see a California, Colorado or New York license plate as you are Georgia or Tennessee. The dense concentration of quality bouldering at this park near Steele attracts rock climbers from around the U.S., and indeed the world; the unique nature of the carved sandstone—a sea of slopers and menacing top outs, in climber-speak—is said to be rivaled in class only by the boulder fields of Fontainebleau, just outside Paris. But before Southern legend Adam Henry established climbing here, there was music. Bluegrass has bounced around the park's natural amphitheater for decades, with up to 10,000 revelers gathering in days gone by to hear the likes of Bill Monroe, Lester Flatt and Earl Scruggs. It is claimed that a 16-year-old Emmylou Harris made her first public appearance here, playing barefoot onstage. The park's current owners have brought the music back, with bluegrass gatherings throughout the year.

"DAMN THE TORPEDOES"

Legend has it these words were uttered by Rear Admiral David G. Farragut in the late stages of the Civil War while leading his fleet in to take back Mobile Bay for the United States. In the early light of August 5, 1864, he had just seen the USS *Tecumseh* collide with one of 67 mines stretched across the mouth of the bay between Fort Gaines and Fort Morgan. The iron-sided monitor ship sank within two minutes. As the rest of his ships slowed and the Confederate guns rang out, a furious Farragut cried out his mythical words before sailing to victory: "Damn the torpedoes! Full speed ahead!" More than a century later, this moment would find a rock-and-roll echo: After fighting his record label and the conventions of the music industry throughout its making, Tom Petty tapped into Mobile Bay lore to name the Heartbreakers' classic third album and capture the single-minded focus and swagger the moment required: *Damn the Torpedoes.*

SOUTHERN LIVING

1886 .... Leonidas LaFayette Polk, a Confederate veteran, publishes *The Progressive Farmer*, a weekly newsletter in North Carolina

1890s ... Newsletter becomes magazine, official publication of the National Farmers' Alliance and Industrial Union

1911 ...... Magazine moves headquarters to Birmingham; name of publisher changes to Progressive Farmer Company

1930 ..... *Progressive Farmer* merges with *Southern Ruralist*, bringing subscribership to one million

1960s ... As the number of family farms drops, company aims to expand readership with a magazine focused on gardens, food, travel and regional happenings

1966 ..... *Southern Living* debuts, in era marked by civil-rights activism and media change; doubles circulation within two years

1979 ..... *Southern Living* begins *Southern Living* Annual Recipes books

1980 ..... Progressive Farmer Company changes name to Southern Progress Corporation. Subscription rate reaches 2 million; among top 15 nationally in monthly advertising revenue.

1985 ..... Time Inc. buys Southern Progress for $480 million, its first publication purchase and largest sum ever for a magazine at the time

1987 ..... Southern Progress launches *Cooking Light*, spinning off *Southern Living* column

2017 ..... Time Inc. moves *Food & Wine* offices to Birmingham. Meredith Corporation purchases Time Inc.

THE PROGRESSIVE FARMER, JULY 1918. *Do you remember the little boy's pathetic lament in Riley's Griggsby Station, the little boy who had moved from the farm to the so-called fine home in the crowded city: "What in all this grand life and high situation / And mary pink nor hollyhock bloomin' at the door." Anyhow, we are reminded that this is the month to plant hollyhocks for next spring's blooming and millions of them ought to be planted by our readers. They can be had in almost all colors, require very little care, and bloom profusely and gloriously the whole summer long.*

WRITERS OF NOTE

HARPER LEE Hometown Monroeville—and the real-life 1931 Scottsboro trial—threads through seminal *To Kill a Mockingbird.*

ZORA NEALE HURSTON Notasulga-born folklorist-anthropologist's *Their Eyes Were Watching God,* rendered in Southern Black vernacular, a jewel of American and Harlem Renaissance literature.

FANNIE FLAGG Actress and Oscar-nommed writer's *Fried Green Tomatoes at the Whistle Stop Cafe* was inspired by an Irondale meat and three.

MARGARET RENKL Prolific backyard naturalist was born in Andalusia; essays *Late Migrations* contain the roads, riverbeds, relationships of her early life.

ALBERT MURRAY Tuskegee classmate of Ralph Ellison and author of *The Omni-Americans,* he wrote on race relations, the Blues and jazz.

YAA GYASI Iowa Writers' Workshop-ordained author of much-lauded *Homegoing* was born in Ghana and Rocket City raised.

TRUMAN CAPOTE Author of legendary works like *Breakfast at Tiffany's* and *In Cold Blood* began writing alongside childhood neighbor and longtime friend Harper Lee.

RICK BRAGG Pulitzer Prize-winning feature writer recounts his tempestuous Piedmont youth in *All Over but the Shoutin'.*

HELEN KELLER Attended Radcliffe College and graduated as the first deafblind person to earn a bachelor's degree. Born in Tuscumbia, she published 12 books including *The Story of My Life* in 1903 at age 22.

BRYAN STEVENSON *Just Mercy* is a call to action to end mass incarceration from the lawyer and MacArthur genius who founded Equal Justice Initiative.

ZELDA FITZGERALD Montgomery-born novelist's *Save Me the Waltz* is laced with Alabama memories.

E.O. WILSON His Birmingham childhood sparked deep curiosity in nature, yielded much-lauded *On Human Nature, The Ants* and two Pulitzers.

FIGHT SONGS

UNIVERSITY OF ALABAMA

Written by Ethelred "Epp" Sykes, editor of the Crimson White, *following the school's first national championship in the Rose Bowl in 1926.*

Yea, Alabama! Drown 'em, Tide!
Every 'Bama man's behind you,
Hit your stride.
Go teach the Bulldogs to behave,
Send the Yellow Jackets to a watery grave.
And if a man starts to weaken,
That's a shame!
For 'Bama's pluck and grit have
Writ her name in Crimson flame.
Fight on, fight on, fight on, men!
Remember the Rose Bowl, we'll win then.
So roll on to victory,
Hit your stride,
You're Dixie's football pride,
Crimson Tide, Roll Tide, Roll Tide!!

AUBURN UNIVERSITY

Commissioned by Auburn supporter Roy B. Sewell, written by New York songwriters Robert Allen and Al Stillman, for the 1955 season.

War Eagle, fly down the field
Ever to conquer, never to yield
War Eagle, fearless and true
Fight on, you orange and blue
Go! Go! Go!
On to vict'ry, strike up the band
Give 'em hell, give 'em hell
Stand up and yell, hey!
War Eagle, win for Auburn,
Power of Dixieland!

TUSKEGEE UNIVERSITY

Booker T. Washington asked Paul Laurence Dunbar, America's most famous Black poet at the time, to write a piece for the school's 25th anniversary in 1906. The accompanying tune was composed by Nathaniel Clark Smith, Tuskegee Institute band director from 1906-1913.

I

Tuskegee, thou pride of the swift growing South
We pay thee our homage today
For the worth of thy teaching, the joy of thy care;
And the good we have known 'neath thy sway.
Oh, long-striving mother of diligent sons
And of daughters whose strength is their pride,
We will love thee forever and ever shall walk
Thro' the oncoming years at thy side.

II

Thy Hand we have held up the difficult steeps,
When painful and slow was the pace,
And onward and upward we've labored with thee
For the glory of God and our race.
The fields smile to greet us, the forests are glad,
The ring of the anvil and hoe
Have a music as thrilling and sweet as a harp
Which thou taught us to hear and to know.

III

Oh, mother Tuskegee, thou shinest today
As a gem in the fairest of lands;
Thou gavest the Heav'n-blessed power to see
The worth of our minds and our hands.
We thank thee, we bless thee, we pray for thee years
Imploring with grateful accord,
Full fruit for thy striving, time longer to strive,
Sweet love and true labor's reward.

INCLUDED

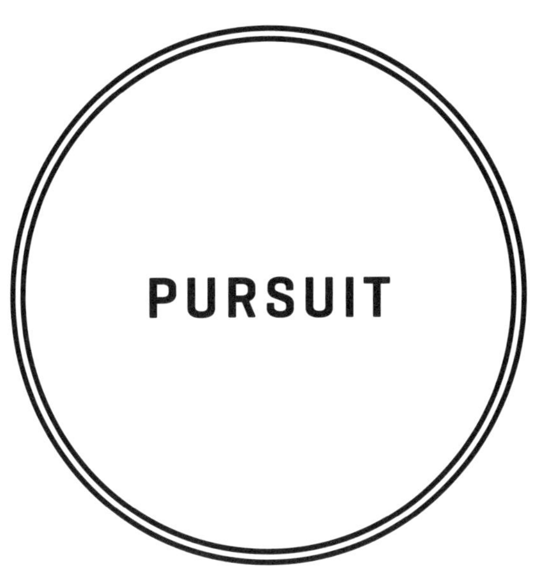

A field guide to music in Alabama with historical insight, playlists [with listening notes] and sites to hear, learn, create

MUSIC IN ALABAMA

Alabama's music is as diverse as its geography: From Appalachian foothills, where Randy Owen and ALABAMA created their own brand of "mountain music," to Birmingham's urbane jazz legacy and, later, DIY punk scene. These mountains' taper has sheltered musical minds from "Father of the Blues" W.C. HANDY to country avatar HANK WILLIAMS.

This sweeping creativity speaks of histories embodied in sound, reflecting mingled legacies of free and enslaved Africans, bygone Irish immigration, country living and industrial labor. For all the importance of the past, the state continues to propel music forward. It could be said that music makes Alabama a crossroads of modern art.

Before Florence's SAM PHILLIPS recorded Elvis Presley at Sun Studios in Memphis, BIG MAMA THORNTON from Ariton pressed "Hound Dog" to vinyl. In the 1960s, RICK HALL's Florence Alabama Music Enterprises [FAME] became one of the most in-demand studios in America. It was home to sessions with Arthur Alexander, Wilson Pickett and Clarence Carter, among others, before Aretha Franklin arrived and found her sound backed by session band, THE SWAMPERS. Those players [Barry Beckett, Roger Hawkins, David Hood, Jimmy Johnson] later created a studio of their own across the river: MUSCLE SHOALS SOUND STUDIO, where the Rolling Stones came to record some of their most iconic songs.

Alabama is a bastion of SACRED HARP church singing, and home of the first American city to host a Mardi Gras celebration, held 1703 in Mobile. Here, the horns of EXCELSIOR BAND have kept the party popping since 1883. The state is also home to country duo THE LOUVIN BROTHERS, who explored the boundaries of the secular and nonsecular, set against the gothic South they were raised in. Later, the Drive-By Truckers, fronted by Patterson Hood, son of The Swampers' David, would carve their own rock sound with similar themes: a band rebelling against home, fighting for what they saw as right. Their punk ethos—with a drawl—helped create an entire genre of country music misfits, blanketed under the term "Americana."

Heritage can shift across time and family trees, across generations and styles. Somehow, Alabama music is always Alabama music, a wellspring of national and global sounds.

ALABAMA MUSIC HISTORY

c. 1500s Yuchi people migrate to what is now the Tennessee River ………. region in Northern Alabama, which they called "nunnuhsae," meaning "singing river"

1600s-… Enslaved Africans, bringing banjo and spirituals, and waves 1800s of Scots-Irish people with fiddle music, build foundations of region's traditional music

1703 ….. First Carnival and Mardi Gras observance in Mobile

1841 ….. Coosa County publication of *The Primitive Hymns*, religious poetry without music notes, pre-dating shape-note book *The Sacred Harp* [1844]

1870s …. Industrialization brings labor songs of coal mines, steel mills, railroad, Mobile docks

1873 …… W.C. Handy, "Father of Blues," born in Florence

1881 ….. Birth of James Reese Europe in Mobile. Pianist Eubie Blake later calls the ragtime and jazz innovator the "Martin Luther King of music."

1883 ….. Marching jazz outfit Excelsior Band forms in Mobile

1902 ….. Birth of Adele "Vera" Hall, foremost singer of blues and African American spirituals, with long-reaching influence. [Moby's 1999 album *Play* incorporates Hall's "Trouble So Hard."]

1926 ….. Hank Williams Sr., age three, watches mother play organ at Mount Olive Baptist Church

1952 …… Big Mama Thornton of Ariton/Montgomery records "Hound Dog," four years before Elvis

1959 ….. Rick Hall and Billy Sherrill partner with Tom Stafford to launch publishing company Florence Alabama Music Enterprises [FAME]

1969 ….. FAME signs Capitol Records deal. Muscle Sound Rhythm Section [The Swampers] leave to open Muscle Shoals Sound Studio. Both studios prosper through 1970s.

1978 …… Swampers leave their original studio, which becomes an appliance store. Owner leaves the control-room glass, cabinets, vocal booth, furniture intact.

2013 …… Premiere of *Muscle Shoals* documentary. Dr. Dre's Beats donates $1 million to Muscle Shoals Sound Studio for reopening.

2017 …… Muscle Shoals Sound Studio reopens with a first session: The Black Keys' Dan Auerbach

ALABAMA PLAYLIST

W.C. HANDY *"St. Louis Blues,"* 1914 Florence-born, "Father of Blues." Listen for: Handy's aim [as written in his autobiography]: "To combine ragtime syncopation with a real melody in the spiritual tradition."

HANK WILLIAMS WITH HIS DRIFTING COWBOYS *"Kaw-Liga,"* 1953 Choosing one song from the son of Mount Olive who defined country music is ... difficult. This one, written with Fred Rose, is iconic. Listen for: Forlorn minor key modulating to major at chorus.

ERSKINE HAWKINS *"Tuxedo Junction,"* 1939 Hawkins led a Birmingham jazz movement centered around the venue that shares a name with this tune. Listen for: Lyrics by Buddy Feyne, inspired by Hawkins' explanation of the Junction's role as a stop on the Chitlin' Circuit, a collection of venues welcoming to Black folks during segregation.

SUN RA *"Space is the Place,"* 1974 While space may have been the place for his story, his roots were Magic City. Listen for: The pathways this jazz experiment opened for the avant rock likes of Sonic Youth and Primal Scream.

PERCY SLEDGE *"When a Man Loves a Woman,"* 1966 Leighton-born hospital orderly finds stardom his first time in the studio. Listen for: A 15-year-old Doris Allen's backing vocals, which earned her $15.50 for the session.

WILSON PICKETT *"Hey Jude,"* 1969 Jimmy Johnson of the Muscle Shoals Rhythm Section called it the beginning of Southern rock. Listen for: Prattville native's vocals, with guitar wails by Duane Allman, then a session player who sometimes slept at FAME.

ALABAMA *"Tennessee River,"* 1979 First #1 hit from the Fort Payne group. Listen for: Jeff Cook's fiddle at the bridge, tribute to band's mountain home.

THE TEMPTATIONS *"Get Ready,"* 1966 Last song written and produced by Smokey Robinson. Listen for: Birmingham native Eddie Kendricks on lead.

COMMODORES, *"Brick House,"* 1977 Hitmakers began their career while students at the Tuskegee Institute. Listen for: Lionel Richie on saxophone, drummer Walter Orange singing lead.

LYNYRD SKYNYRD *"Free Bird,"* 1973 Florida band inextricably linked to Alabama. Listen for: Iconic piano by keyboardist Billy Powell, a classically trained player who suggested the part while working as their roadie.

BIG MAMA THORNTON *"Hound Dog,"* 1952 Elvis Presley launched a career with it in 1956, but Thornton, of Ariton, Alabama, cut it first in 1952. Listen for: Sparse arrangement, unlike other R&B records at the time, and guitar as a main element, laying groundwork for rock and roll.

THE STAPLE SINGERS *"I'll Take You There,"* 1972 "The epitome of the Muscle Shoals Sound." —David Fricke, *Rolling Stone*. Listen for: That bass line, one of the best in music history, by David Hood.

THE LOUVIN BROTHERS/EMMYLOU HARRIS *"If I Could Only Win Your Love,"* 1958/1975 The Henagar, Alabama, brothers recorded it in 1958; the Birmingham-born songbird in 1975. Listen for: Harris' harmonies with banjo-playing Herb Pedersen.

DRIVE-BY TRUCKERS *"TVA" and "Uncle Frank,"* 2009, 1999 Jason Isbell-penned "TVA" and Mike Cooley-penned "Uncle Frank" paint pictures of Northwest Alabama in late 20th century. Listen for: Lyrical storytelling.

THE O-JAYS *"For the Love of Money,"* 1973 The name comes from 1 Timothy 6:10: "For the love of money is the root of all evil." [Later the theme for reality TV's *The Apprentice*.] Listen for: Frontman Eddie Levert of Bessemer.

JASON ISBELL AND THE 400 UNIT *"Alabama Pines,"* 2011 Like an unofficial Alabama state song. Listen for: Isbell giving directions in the second verse, setting scenes that show a deep affinity for place.

ARTHUR ALEXANDER/THE ROLLING STONES *"You Better Move On,"* 1964 Originally by Alexander of Sheffield, in early days of FAME as it needed a lift in business. At Muscle Shoals Sound Studio, The Stones cut "You Gotta Move" and massive hits "Wild Horses" and "Brown Sugar." Listen for: Alexander's soulful sound, an inspiration for The Stones.

ARETHA FRANKLIN *"I Never Loved a Man [The Way I Love You],"* 1967 Queen of Soul found breakout sound in tumultuous Shoals sessions. Listen for: Session player Spooner Oldham's opening Wurlitzer riff, which broke a moment of studio writers' block.

MUSIC SITES OF ALABAMA

FAME RECORDING STUDIOS

Between a pharmacy and a liquor store, find Florence Alabama Music Enterprises, second and current home of producer Rick Hall's empire, where Etta James, Wilson Pickett, Aretha Franklin, among others, recorded. 603 *Avalon Ave, Muscle Shoals*

SUN RA'S GRAVE

Sun Ra [Herman Blount] crash-landed from outer space in Birmingham, as the story goes. The jazz visionary ultimately came to rest at Elmwood Cemetery & Mausoleum. 600 *Martin Luther King Jr Dr, Birmingham*

MOBILE CARNIVAL MUSEUM

Celebrating 300 years of history in the South's birthplace of Mardi Gras. 355 *Government St, Mobile*

ALABAMA JAZZ HALL OF FAME

Connected to the retrofitted Carver Theatre and forthcoming Birmingham Black Radio Museum. 1701 *4th Ave N, Birmingham*

W.C. HANDY BIRTHPLACE, MUSEUM AND LIBRARY

Built by his grandfather, the modest, restored log cabin marks the place where William Charles Handy was born in 1873. It houses a large collection of sheet music and papers as well as the piano of the songwriter, arranger and publisher. 620 *W College St, Florence*

MUSCLE SHOALS SOUND STUDIO
Studio of The Swampers after leaving FAME. Legendary Rolling Stones sessions. More recently: Band of Horses, Chris Stapleton. *3614 Jackson Hwy N, Sheffield*

THE ORION AMPHITHEATER
Greek-style amphitheater for major touring acts. *701 Amphitheater Dr NW, Huntsville*

THE NICK
"Birmingham's Dirty Little Secret," capacity 300. Drive-By Truckers to Widespread Panic. *2514 10th Ave S, Birmingham*

HANK WILLIAMS SITES
Museum [118 Commerce St, Montgomery], gravesite [1304 Upper Wetumpka Rd, Montgomery] and The Redmont Hotel in Birmingham, where he spent his final night. *2101 5th Ave N, Birmingham.*

STANDARD DELUXE
Club in rural Waverly [population 152] just outside Auburn hosts a slew of indie acts: Alabama Shakes, St. Paul & the Broken Bones and more. *1015 Mayberry Ave, Waverly*

ALABAMA MUSIC HALL OF FAME Honorees range from Hank Williams to Donna Jean Godchaux of the Grateful Dead. *617 U.S. 72 W, Tuscumbia*

PLACES OF NOTE

MUSIC VENUES

LAVA ROOM
1401 *Huntsville Rd, Florence*
Compelling shows, strong leadership. [Ramen shop too!]

AVONDALE BREWING COMPANY
201 *41st St S, Birmingham*
Top-notch outdoor setup, holds 2,000.

THREE CAVES
901 *Kennamer Dr SE, Huntsville*
Listen between the walls of a reclaimed limestone quarry.

ALABAMA MUSIC BOX
12 *S Conception St, Mobile*
Reincarnation of Mobtown anti-establishment establishment.

SATURN
200 *41st St S Birmingham*
Outer-space-themed, local and touring acts.

ALABAMA THEATRE
1817 *3rd Ave N, Birmingham*
Historic venue hosting national acts.

OAK MOUNTAIN AMPHITHEATRE
500 *23rd St S, Birmingham*
Largest outdoor venue in the state.

LYRIC THEATRE
1800 *3rd Ave N, Birmingham*
Since 1914, vaudeville to modern day.

RECORDING STUDIOS

WISHBONE
Part of Shoals studio legacy since 1972.

THE NUTTHOUSE
Founded by Jimmy Nutt, Grammy-winning engineer.

RECORD SHOPS

10,000 HZ RECORDS
717*A First Ave, Opelika*

DR. MUSIC
35 *S Section St, Fairhope*

NU WAY VINYL
2404 *Woodward Ave Muscle Shoals*

OZ MUSIC
506 *14th St Tuscaloosa*

SEASICK RECORDS
4420 *4th Ave S Birmingham*

VERTICAL HOUSE RECORDS
2211 *Seminole Dr SW, Huntsville*

MORE ALABAMA MUSIC INSPIRATION

see also pages 14, 70, 77

BIRMINGHAM .... Randy Newman
SONG OF THE SOUTH .... Alabama
ALABAMA WALTZ ..... Hank Williams
ALABAMA GETAWAY ... Grateful Dead
SEA STAR .... St. Paul and Broken Bones
ALABAMA RAIN .... Jim Croce
MOBILE BLUE .... John Mellencamp
TRAIN TO BIRMINGHAM ..... John Hiatt

THE SHOALS: A GLOSSARY

RICK HALL Born into rural poverty, picked up a mandolin at age 6. Later founded FAME Studios.

140B WURLITZER Electric piano, sharp sound. FAME studios still uses the one Spooner Oldham played on Aretha Franklin's "I Never Loved a Man": recorded in about 15 minutes. Original Hammond B3s, too.

JERRY WEXLER Said to have coined the term "rhythm and blues," 1947, while a reporter for *Billboard*. As Atlantic Records executive, befriended Hall, then fell out over an Aretha session. Flew Hall's Muscle Shoals Rhythm Section to New York to finish the record, and later backed the players when they opened Muscle Shoals Sound Studio [MSSS] across town.

3614 JACKSON HIGHWAY Street address of Muscle Shoals Sound Studio and name of 1969 Wexler-produced Cher album, the first recorded in the space. Studio sign was photo-edited onto album cover; actual sign debuted in 1970.

MUSCLE SHOALS RHYTHM SECTION Leon Russell's producer described these session players as having a "swampy sound." Liner notes dubbed them "The Swampers." Later came Lynyrd Skynyrd lyric: "Now Muscle Shoals has got The Swampers." Players include Jimmy Johnson, Hall's first employee at FAME [engineered The Stones at 24]; bassist David Hood, who met Jimmy Johnson at Sheffield Junior High; Roger Hawkins, Greenhill native who played drums on "Respect" at age 19; Barry Beckett, Birmingham-born keyboard player, arranger and only member of the section who read music.

KODACHROME Nickname Johnson gave the MSSS Yamaha baby grand piano. Heard on Bob Seger's "Old Time Rock and Roll," Willie Nelson's "Bloody Mary Morning," and of course, Paul Simon's "Kodachrome."

MSSS BATHROOM Small wood-paneled room where a black-painted toilet seat hangs over the door like a good-luck horseshoe. Richards locked himself in and finished "Wild Horses." Duane Allman preferred recording in here. Mary MacGregor sang hit "Torn Between Two Lovers" while avoiding her own reflection in the bathroom mirror.

Rising

PROTEST SONGS

MISSISSIPPI GODDAMN *Nina Simone, 1964* Written partly in response to the 16th Street Baptist Church bombing that killed four young girls in Birmingham.

ALABAMA *John Coltrane, 1963* Inspired by Martin Luther King Jr.'s speech following the 16th Street bombing, with phrasing that follows his speech patterns. No words necessary.

I SHALL NOT BE MOVED *Ella Fitzgerald, 1967* Anthem of the civil rights movement; covered by many, including Mavis Staples.

BIRMINGHAM SUNDAY *Joan Baez, 1964* Written by Richard Fariña, Baez's brother-in-law, in wake of 16th Street Baptist bombing.

GLORY *Common & John Legend, 2015* Connects Selma marches to Ferguson, Missouri.

A CHANGE IS GONNA COME *Sam Cooke, 1964* Inspired in part by Cooke's experience of racism in cities like Shreveport and Birmingham, and by Bob Dylan's "Blowin' in the Wind."

DERECONSTRUCTED *Lee Bains III & the Glory Fires, 2014* Band formed in Birmingham, album full of fire. Leads with image of white supremacist Bull Conner in a church.

THOUGHTS AND PRAYERS *Drive-By Truckers, 2020* Never ones to shy away from social issues, this track takes on gun violence.

ALABAMA *Neil Young, 1972* Follow up to his "Southern Man"; the songs elicited a response from Lynyrd Skynyrd in the form of "Sweet Home Alabama."

13TH CENTURY METAL *Brittany Howard, 2019* A manifesto on love, equality, from Alabama Shakes singer's solo debut.

TAKE ME TO THE SPEEDWAY *Dexateens, 2005* The band formed in Tuscaloosa takes a stand against the Confederate flag.

WHITE MAN'S WORLD *Jason Isbell and the 400 Unit, 2017* A confrontation of privilege by son of Green Hill.

FOREVER BLACK AMERICA AGAIN *Gucci Mane/Common/Pusha T/BJ The Chicago Kid, 2016* Gucci Mane of Bessemer raps about the Black experience.

INCLUDED

INTERVIEWS

Ten conversations with locals of note about Alabama music, food, football and working toward space travel

JASON ISBELL

SONGWRITER

MY GRANDMOTHER worked at the cafeteria at the high school next door to their house, and she would bring home those drop cookies, chocolate and oatmeal.

I REMEMBER WAITING in the door of the trailer for her red Ford Maverick. I was probably 2.

I DON'T FEEL like I'm qualified to sing R&B music or Blues music. Otherwise, that's what I'd be doing, probably. But rock and roll is sort of made for people like me.

EVERYTHING I DO is heavily influenced by the impressions I took from the music that was made in Muscle Shoals.

I THINK IT'S as good as American art ever got. I don't think you're going to find a painting or book or movie or another song that's better than Otis Redding or Aretha.

THE TECHNOLOGICAL limitations they had at that time gave everything a sort of humanity.

THE RECORDINGS sounded like they were played by people in a room together, because it just naturally happened.

THEY WEREN'T USING as many microphones and Pro Tools and Auto-Tune. They were trying to play it as clean and as slick as they could in the timeframe they had. Usually they were cutting two tracks a day or more.

I THINK THEY did "Mustang Sally" and "Land of 1000 Dances" in the same day for Pickett.

BEFORE THERE WAS a sort of monopoly on radio, concert venues, tickets and every aspect of the music business, you had more room to be creative.

YOU COULD AIM for a hit and wind up with a really, really good song, which is much harder to do now.

NOW, if you want to write something that actually moves people, you have to be resigned to not selling as many copies.

DAVID HOOD TOLD me once, "Make sure all your gear works and show up on time and you'll be ahead of 90 percent of the musicians in the world." And he was right.

IN A METAPHORICAL sense, I'm writing about where I'm from and where I am, in all of the different ways.

IT'S VERY RARE I write a song that doesn't include some kind of location.

IF I SAY the word "Alabama" in a song, there are four or five things I could mean by that. Then I can use the rest of the song to show you which version of Alabama I'm talking about here.

THE SKYNYRD VERSION and the Neil Young version are polar opposites, and then there's all kinds of stuff in the middle.

IN A SONG, you only have three or four minutes to do the work.

I TALK ABOUT time and growth and how to succeed at becoming a better person. That's something you're not going to be able to talk about unless you can set the context of where you came from in all the different ways. The easiest way to skip to that is to say, "This is the place where I came from."

THE JOB REALLY is to remind people of what we have in common. I think that's what the better songwriters do.

SO, WHEN YOU'RE in the middle of Oklahoma for a few months and start talking to people and notice they aren't very different from the folks you grew up around, then you say, "Here's an opportunity to do that job."

I'VE LEARNED PEOPLE are very similar from place to place, in positive and negative ways.

YOU HEAR GROWING up that the bad bigotry happens more often in the South, but it happens all over the place.

THE POSITIVE THINGS are widespread too.

THE CLOSE FAMILY bonds we had growing up in smalltown Alabama are reflected in the biggest cities.

I'M REMINDED OF that with immigrant families who all live under the same roof in New York or Los Angeles, staying close to each other for survival.

ROSCOE HALL

CHEF, PAINTER

I HAVE 27 years of professional cooking, so it's still in me to say "chef." But I have to start saying I'm an artist now.

MY ART, RECENTLY, is informed by the Black Belt region.

FOR MY PAINTINGS, I use things indigenous to there. The soil. Old seeds. I've been dehydrating sweet potatoes to make pigments. I make charcoal from pecan and hickory wood, like they use at Dreamland Barbecue.

MY MOM'S DAD is John C. Bishop, who started it in 1956 in Tuscaloosa. The original cafe was burned down by the KKK in '53 and he rebuilt it. It started out with fried fish sandwiches and hamburgers. My grandmother came from a Haitian slave family in the Low Country, so she incorporated allspice into what is now known as Dreamland's spicy barbecue sauce.

IN '96, I was like, *I gotta get to California and learn how to cook all this beautiful food.* Frank Stitt wrote a reference letter for me at Chez Panisse.

I WAS STAYING on people's couches the majority of the time I worked there. But when I had enough to get an apartment, I didn't want to live there anymore. I went to Portland, Oregon. I got my undergraduate in photography, and took pictures for a skateboarding magazine.

I LIVE IN Mountain Brook now, and it feels like I'm the only Black dude. But everyone knows me because they're like, "Oh you're on *Top Chef*!" or "You cooked at my house before!"

STILL, I THINK Alabama is a bit more progressive than people think. Since the '50s and '60s, I feel like people learned to live with each other in comparison to other cities.

I LIKE ALABAMA. My family is here. I have old memories here.

BUT I'M FINALLY making some new ones.

DAVID HOOD

BASSIST

I STARTED PLAYING the trombone in high school band about the same time I started playing bass guitar. The bass is a certain frequency sound, and trombone is too. They're both bass-clef instruments.

I'VE ALWAYS LOVED music, and I just fell into it. I didn't plan on it. My father had a tire store. I worked there and was playing on weekends—little frat-party-type gigs. Pretty soon, I just got very, very busy in the studio.

AT FIRST, I did a few sessions in Nashville. But we got so busy in Muscle Shoals I was not going to Nashville very much unless it was something big.

WHEN OUR rhythmic section was together, it developed a sound of its own without us even trying. We had different lead guitar players. Eddie Hinton was one, and later, Pete Carr. It was mainly just myself, Roger Hawkins, Barry Beckett on keys to begin with, and Jimmy Johnson on rhythm guitar.

WE WERE ALL very close friends and worked just about every day together. Unfortunately, everybody's gone now but me.

WE WORKED WITH white people and Black people, and race never made a bit of difference. I always liked the way Black players played, and I liked the way they sing. It was always one of the better parts of what I do—working with different races and people, men, women, everything.

WE DID A lot of rhythm and blues. I think every one of us, our favorite music was Black music. We started doing Rod Stewart and Paul Simon, who are white guys, and I'm a white guy, but I've always just been in love with Black music. And a lot of people would come to us and would be surprised that we were white.

WE REALLY NEVER tried to have a sound of our own. If we worked with Paul Simon, we tried to make it sound like we were his band. The same with Luther Ingram or anybody else.

"I'LL TAKE YOU THERE," by The Staple Singers, was just one key, one song.

IT WAS IN C, so you go to A, F, C, that kind of thing. Over and over, except when we got to the little instrumental section. I don't really remember how we worked that up. We kind of worked it up together, the instrumental section. It's hard to describe music.

I ALWAYS TRY to come up with a bassline that has a substance, not just a *boom, boom, boom, boom,* that kind of thing. It does something, and it's almost like a melody.

APRIL HENDERSON

CRIMSONETTE COACH

IN MY LIFE, I've only missed about five home football games.

I'M FROM A small town north of Tuscaloosa, but my mom and dad had season tickets.

WE HAD A motor home, and we tailgated.

AFTER GAMES, my grandfather would grill a steak for everybody in our family. Sometimes the games wouldn't be over until 9 p.m., but it didn't matter. There were 25 or 30 of us eating a steak dinner.

I KNEW FROM an early age I wanted to be a Crimsonette or a cheerleader. I started taking dance lessons when I turned three and baton in kindergarten.

AFTER MY TIME on the line, I stayed connected to the program, and in 2019, the former coach retired and I took over.

BAND CAMP IS three times a day for two weeks. Once school starts, we practice six days a week. It's a lot of work.

THE MAIN THING I want from them when they leave me is a ton of confidence. Not cocky but confident—because they're going to need it.

I ALWAYS TELL them, "The world is waiting to tell you you're not enough. But when you leave me, I want to build you up so high it's going to take a whole lot to bring you down."

THE BAND HAS been around over 100 years, and Crimsonettes a part of the band for 53 years.

CARLA AND CHRISTIE were the first Crimsonette sister act. They twirled in the '80s. In the late '90s, their cousin Cay came along. Christie passed away of breast cancer while in her early 40s. Courtney, Christie's daughter, came around 2012. Now my captain on the line is Caroline, Carla's daughter.

THEY ALL COME together on Alumni Day. They always say that Christie is with them when they march together.

BRENDA WADE

NASA SPECIALIST

I WENT TO work on May 20, 1968. Right after high school I took the civil service test, and I got hired.

I WORKED MY way up to a launch operations support specialist. I started as a GS2 clerk typist, and when I retired, top step of a GS13.

I'M PROBABLY CLOSE to the longest-tenured employee at NASA. Almost 53 years.

I WORKED AT Marshall Space Flight Center, and I worked at the Huntsville Operations Support Center, where we did all the shuttle launches.

THE BEST JOB in the world was the one where I worked at the HOSC. Today, I still have an astronaut friend. He calls me on my birthday. Where else could you work that you've got an astronaut friend?

THE GROUND SHOOK under your feet with the Apollo launch, more so than the shuttle launch. But I worked on all of them. It was just so exciting.

YOU GET BY with your friends. If I didn't know the answer to something, they did. They help you out, and you help them out.

I SAID, "I'm not an electrician, but I know how to coordinate and get things done." I was in charge of a $6.5-million project, and that was just making a computer room, electrically and mechanically. And I was the only female in that meeting with all the men.

I WORKED HERE when von Braun was center director, the first center director we ever had. Today, Jody Singer, a female, is the center director. So you see how that evolved over the years.

OF COURSE, I also worked with Ann McNair—she was our lab director at one time.

SHE TOLD ME, "Brenda, I don't know how you get things done, but I'm not going to change anything."

CYNTHIA TUCKER

JOURNALIST

I GRADUATED FROM Auburn University in 1976. I got hired right out of college at the old *Atlanta Journal*. I didn't ever intend to live in Alabama again, because of what Alabama was like then.

I WAS WRITING columns twice a week. But my predecessor, the late, great Ralph McGill, who also won a Pulitzer, wrote every day. My goodness.

ALABAMA HAS CHANGED a lot. My hometown, Monroeville, elected its first Black mayor.

AT THE UNIVERSITY of South Alabama I teach journalism. I teach in the English and political science departments.

FRYE GAILLARD and I wrote a book of essays together, *The Southernization of America: A Story of Democracy in the Balance*.

THIS IS NOT an exact quote, but we quote the late, great John Lewis saying if there was hope for the United States anywhere, it lay in the South.

I THINK THE reason he said that was because the South has had to grapple with the nation's original sin, slavery and racism, in a more direct way than the rest of the nation ever has had to.

WE HAVE MADE so much progress in the South it's not going to be possible to turn back the clock.

I DON'T THINK most people—Black, white or brown—want to turn back the clock. And I think the South can teach the rest of the nation lessons about how to deal with issues of race and diversity.

I GREW UP under the shadow of Jim Crow. I remember when Black people couldn't use the same public restrooms or sit down in most restaurants.

MY STUDENTS HAVE always grown up going to school with people of different races. Diversity of all kinds, and they're comfortable with it. The idea that a classroom or workplace should not be diverse would not have occurred to them.

PARDIS STITT

RESTAURATEUR

I REMEMBER 30 years ago, talking to the staff at Highlands, saying the people who come to our restaurants are the people who live here.

THERE'S A CERTAIN gravitas that comes with that. It's our responsibility to look after them.

WE HAVE THIS advantage of being in a smaller town. We're not a convention center, where thousands of people come through, you see them one time and they're gone.

IT WILL NOW be 41 years ago when Highlands first opened. There were country clubs. John's Seafood was downtown. There was Joy Young Restaurant. So when Highlands opened, it was pretty revolutionary, I think, to have this restaurant with a French-leaning chef using Southern regional ingredients.

I WAS BORN in Texas but pretty much grew up in Birmingham. I went to school here and never thought I would stay. I'm so glad I did.

A GOOD FRIEND of mine was working in a restaurant when I was in college. They were short-staffed. She was the manager and needed help on the door. I didn't know what that meant, but she said she could teach me. She asked me again the next week. I was hooked.

PEOPLE ARE GOOD. People need to have a sense of belonging.

COMING UP AT Bottega Café is kind of our ode to Niki's West. It's the farmers market vegetable plate. We'll have it through summer, then adapt it to more fall-like vegetables.

LADY PEAS, COLLARD greens, creamed corn. Stewed okra and tomatoes. Cornbread with jalapeño, a cucumber-and-tomato salad.

IT'S ONE OF those things, to me, that speaks to time and place and the summer. And what an incredible, hot Alabama summer can produce.

SCOTT PEACOCK

CHEF

THE FIRST Biscuit Experience was in January 2019. Very soon there will have been 1,200 biscuiteers who have come through.

IT HAS ALWAYS been about story, narrative and place.

WHEN YOU COME to Marion, you've made a journey. That is its own preparation. We're an hour from the nearest interstate. Your route is breathtakingly beautiful and historic. For example, if you're coming from Montgomery, you're driving the march route.

I WONDERED IF it would ever feel familiar, but like biscuits, I don't take this place for granted. There's always some manifestation of the specialness of it.

WHEN I WAS a younger cook, it was much more about being fancy or adding something, stamping myself onto what I was doing. Then I learned this idea of distillation—removal of the extraneous as a creative act.

UNDERSTANDING what's not right is very critical to knowing what is.

GROWING antique wheat with the mentorship of Glenn Roberts of Anson Mills, changed my relationship to flour, my awareness and appreciation for it.

THE BISCUIT, I believe, should express the maker and not be about someone else's standard.

THE GIFT OF *Southern Cooking* has been out 20 years. Judith Jones walked up to us at the end of Miss Edna Lewis's 80th birthday dinner and said, "The two of you should write this book together, and should do it quickly." Seven years and one day later, it came out.

THERE WAS A huge book signing at Borders. Several hundred people turned out. As we were leaving our apartment to go there together, we were able to express that—which I'll never forget—that from now on, there was a document that we had been friends and created this thing together. It means an awful lot to me.

BRYAN STEVENSON

LAWYER, SOCIAL JUSTICE ADVOCATE

MY GRANDMOTHER'S name was Victoria Baylor.

AS A CHILD, people would come to her home, and her father would read the newspaper aloud. She was so proud that her dad, a former slave, was this source of knowledge.

I CANNOT EXPLAIN my status as a lawyer without explaining this legacy and this attention to the power of words to liberate, to inform, to shape.

MY MOTHER WENT into debt to buy us a set of World Book Encyclopedias. My dad worked in a poultry factory.

HAVING PROXIMITY TO inequality awakens something important for a just society.

MY FIRST TRIP to deathrow as a legal intern, that closeness to condemned people, shaped my thinking. I discovered that I could have an impact by simply being present, by showing up, by being proximate.

MY ROLE IS to respond to the legal challenges, but to also represent the hope of justice.

WE ARE ALL more than the worst thing that we have done.

JUSTICE REQUIRES THAT we know the other things that you are. That exploration is how we create a more complete picture of someone's humanity.

WE HAVE NOT told the truth in our society about slavery and lynching and segregation. When we find the courage to do that, we will be amazed at the power it will release.

I FEEL HONORED to live here and struggle in Montgomery.

I AM STANDING on the shoulders of people who frequently had to say, "My head is bloodied but not bowed."

IT'S A PLACE where the opportunity for restoration and change is rich. We don't have to fear confronting this history.

HOSEA LONDON

BAND LEADER

THE EXCELSIOR BAND started in Mobile in 1883. We are celebrating 140 years this year. This may be the oldest continuous marching jazz band in the country.

WE DO MARDI GRAS parades, weddings. We do funerals. We do church services.

I'VE BEEN THERE for 46, 47 years. It's like a lifetime commitment.

THE BAND DOES not have any regular rehearsals. You come in and basically learn the tunes on the performance. We get that level of musicians, who can come in and listen and play.

I GREW UP in Winter Haven, Florida. My school was recruiting band students, because my band director had fourth graders up to 12th. He was his own feeder system. I've been playing since I was in the fourth grade.

I STARTED ON trumpet, but I majored in music. So I play French horn, play a little piano. I played all the instruments you need to be able to play in order to teach.

I ALSO LEARNED about woodwind instruments and strings. You've got to have a pretty wide range if you're going to be either a director or a teacher.

I'M A RETIRED teacher, but I have a group called The Jazz Studio, which are seventh through 12th graders. We teach traditional jazz. This is outside of the school system, more of a community-type program.

I WISH PEOPLE understood the discipline that music brings that can carry over to any other thing you want to do. My students have gone on to be chemical engineers or pre-med.

THE EXCELSIOR BAND was recipient of the National Endowment for the Arts Award for 2022—the only organization in Mobile to ever receive that award. Right now, it is our crowning-glory achievement.

INCLUDED

Essays and poetry by noted voices exploring art, music and life in Alabama

I KNOW A PLACE

Written by **PATTERSON HOOD**

Originally published in Oxford American, *November* 2020

GROWING UP MUSCLE SHOALS

I was riding in the backseat of my godmother's giant Oldsmobile Delta 88 with Sissy, my beloved maternal grandmother, at the wheel and my godmother, Ann Coldiron, in the passenger seat. The radio was on Q107, the 100,000-watt Top 40 station owned by Sam Phillips that blasted my hometown of Florence, Alabama, with all the hits during my childhood [it's still there, blasting away]. The song was "I'll Take You There," the No. 1 song in the nation at the time. The song is rightfully adored. Prince covered it many times during his performances. He was not alone. *Rolling Stone* magazine ranked the song at 281 in their list of the 500 Greatest Songs of All Time. It was the nineteenth-biggest-selling song of 1972. That year, I was in second grade.

"I'll Take You There" sings of a heavenly place where the troubles of its day are swept aside. It's a simple song structurally. A vamp with the title repeated numerous times over an irresistible groove. A reggae-like bass line [influenced heavily from a song called "Liquidator" by the Harry J Allstars] and a very funky beat. The Staple Singers, a longtime family gospel group who had provided music for rallies and marches for Dr. Martin Luther King, were the vocalists. The song provided them with their first crossover secular No. 1 single. The backing group of musicians consisted of a bunch of Alabama white boys who called themselves the Muscle Shoals Rhythm Section. They later came to be known as the Swampers.

I guess it was Sissy who told me that it was my dad playing bass on that song on the radio. In the car that day, I asked her to turn it up and she did. One minute, fourteen seconds into the song, lead singer Mavis Staples introduces the band during a musical breakdown. Barry Beckett

plays a brief but enchanting piano solo as Mavis says, "Barry, Barry, Barry, play your piano now," followed by a short and tasty guitar solo where she calls out her father, Pops Staples, on lead guitar, even though on that particular recording, the lead guitar was actually played by session guitarist Eddie Hinton [her father would be playing it when they performed live]. Then the song seems to transform as the bass player goes up an octave and Mavis calls out, "David. Little David. Easy here, help me now. C'mon Little David. Alright."

I was eight years old when I realized that Little David was my dad.

In the northwest corner of Alabama, there are four towns, three of which, Sheffield, Tuscumbia, and Muscle Shoals, sit nearly connected on the south side of the Tennessee River with only a sign to tell you when you have left one and entered the other. The fourth one, Florence, sits on the north side of the river. It is the biggest of the four towns, although the combined population of the entire metropolitan area is barely 200,000. That is probably close to twice what the population was back in the '70s and '80s when I was growing up there.

Locals can tell you in depth the differences between the four towns [and why they can never unify into one sizable population center that would carry far more political weight in state affairs]. But to most outsiders, the entire region is better known as the Muscle Shoals area [or the Quad Cities].

Although it has come a long way, inching toward some sort of progress, the Shoals area that I grew up in consisted of two "dry" counties [Lauderdale and Colbert], meaning that to buy a beer you either went to a bootlegger or drove fifteen miles to the Tennessee state line, where you could find a few package stores and honky-tonks. To buy liquor you had to drive a good bit farther, an hour, to the closest towns that sold such things. Or, go to the bootlegger, of which there were many.

The Shoals area was as Bible Belt as it got, essentially controlled by one or two churches that worked hard to keep progressive ideas [on race, or gender, or sexuality], liquor, and any semblance of fun at bay. It was also the home of a musical miracle.

Between 1965 and 1982, hundreds of records were cut in Muscle Shoals at one or more of the several studios scattered around. Many of those records became hits, which led to an amazing array of major artists coming to my sleepy hometown to record at one of the humble little recording studios that had popped up there in the wake of a couple of regional soul hits that had come from FAME Studio. In 1966, Percy Sledge recorded "When a Man Loves a Woman" and sold millions of records. Shortly afterward, famed producer and Atlantic Records executive Jerry Wexler brought Wilson Pickett and then Aretha Franklin to town, where they recorded classic hits like "Mustang Sally" and "I Never Loved a Man [the Way I Love You]."

The Rolling Stones, Bob Dylan, Bobby Womack, Etta James, Paul Simon, Simon and Garfunkel, Rod Stewart, Willie Nelson, and Traffic all recorded hits there, as did a slew of soul acts and later country stars. In the late '70s a sign went up declaring Muscle Shoals the HIT RECORDING CAPITAL OF THE WORLD, as more hits were cut there per capita than anywhere else. A record that probably still stands today.

The backing musicians on many of these hits were a bunch of country boys [mostly white] who had learned their instruments in one of the cover bands that played the SEC college circuit in the early '60s. Over time the better players gravitated from frat parties to one of several groups of session players with names like the FAME Gang and the Muscle Shoals Rhythm Section. My father was the bass player in the latter.

He began playing bass guitar professionally in 1966, just a couple of years after I was born. He wasn't quite twenty-three when he played on Percy Sledge's top-five hit "Warm and Tender Love." Soon he was playing sessions, backing up the likes of Aretha Franklin, Wilson Pickett, Etta James, and Clarence Carter. If my dad's career trajectory seemed unlikely, that paled in comparison to the odds of such a thing occurring at all in a small dry county in the Bible Belt. That so many of the most beloved soul hits of the civil rights era came from an integrated group of players just two hours north of Birmingham, where firehoses and police dogs were used against King's marchers, is the kind of plot that's too far-fetched for fiction and too unbelievable to be told without corresponding proof.

I guess I had been told from time to time that my dad was some kind of musician, but I'm sure that it had never quite registered until that fateful ride in the Oldsmobile, even though I had always loved music, especially the Beatles, whose song "She Loves You" was the No. 1 song the day I was born and whose breakup I heard about on the radio around

I'LL TAKE
YOU
THERE
HLRITO

the time I turned six.

I remember my dad's stereo in the den of our house and a record collection that seemed to be at least a thousand strong. Our house had a piano and a Wurlitzer electric piano, a bass guitar and an acoustic guitar, but I never saw my dad playing anything at home besides his records. Men of his time didn't tend to take work home with them. In that way, he was definitely old school.

Even though, on paper, it might seem that I have followed in my father's footsteps, my place in the music business is almost on an opposite end of the spectrum. I play in a touring band that performs our own songs, many of which I write. I play one hundred or so shows a year in multiple continents and have done so for a couple of decades now.

My dad, on the other hand, went to work every day at the same studio, sat in the same chair, and played bass on other people's songs for whatever artist came to town to hire him to do so. He got paid by the hour, usually something on the union scale. He played on many songs that sold in the millions of copies, but he almost never got "points" or a profit share of those hits. "I'll Take You There" was a massive hit record and has since been used in movies and television commercials, but Dad once figured out that he'd been paid less than $2,000 total for his part—the most recognizable instrumental part of the song and one of the most beloved bass parts in modern music. Such is the life of a session player.

In the second grade, I was classmates with the son of one of my dad's partners. Dale and I were best friends that year. I can remember him standing up before the class in show-and-tell and telling everyone that his father was the greatest drummer in the world. His father, Roger Hawkins, is indeed widely considered one of the finest drummers of all time. In addition to the hits he played on with my father, he also played on "When a Man Loves a Woman" recorded by Percy Sledge and "Respect" recorded by Aretha Franklin. Jerry Wexler, who discovered Ray Charles and was responsible for naming the "Rhythm and Blues" chart, shared Dale's assessment of Roger's drumming.

Unfortunately, Dale's proclamation led to a good pummeling on the playground, and I made a note to myself that I wouldn't talk about my dad's occupation at Harlan Elementary School.

My hometown was the kind of deeply conservative place where, upon meeting someone new, often the first question asked was, "What church do you go to?" Most of my classmates had parents significantly

older than mine who were culturally of a very different time and place. To all but my very best friends, what my dad did was a secret, best left unsaid.

Not that I knew much about it. I'd occasionally get little hints of who was in town, usually from my mom, but my dad shared few details about his work and the things that were going on at the studio. I can count on my hands the number of days I spent over there during my childhood. There were memorable exceptions. Linda Ronstadt recorded part of her self-titled solo album in Muscle Shoals and ended up coming over to the house one evening. She and my mom hit it off and stayed in touch for many years, including when she was one of the biggest stars in the world. [I came home from sixth grade one afternoon to find Linda sitting in our den, drinking beer with my mom.] When Bob Dylan came to town [the first time] I had a playdate with his son Jesse, who was probably about seven. Another time, my family had dinner with Bob Seger, who recorded many of his biggest hits with my dad and my dad's partners. Cat Stevens once came by the house to pick up something from my dad.

As I got older, I became obsessed with music, rock & roll in particular, and I wanted to find out as much as I possibly could about this secret world that was happening right under my town's nose. I began hanging out at the two local record stores all I could, endearing myself to the clerks there with my precocious thirst for musical knowledge. I would pocket my lunch money every week and do odd jobs around my uncle's farm to get the latest releases from Elton John, Pink Floyd, Led Zeppelin, and Todd Rundgren. I had well over a hundred albums before sixth grade and more than two hundred and fifty by the time I entered junior high.

The record store clerks were my true lifeline to all of what was happening. Two in particular became sort of professors in my own personal school of rock. Jay Leavitt ran the cool little record store in Muscle Shoals about a block from the original FAME Studios that saw the recording of the classic Aretha and Wilson Pickett sessions. Jay was the one who turned me on to the Rolling Stones and explained what a special occurrence it was having the biggest rock & roll band in the world record three songs—"Brown Sugar," "Wild Horses," and "You Gotta Move"—at my dad's studio. Jay also introduced me to Bruce Springsteen and took me to my first R.E.M. concert. Now, he owns Deep Groove Records in Richmond, Virginia.

The other record store guy was Terrell Benton, who was an assistant manager at the Record Bar in the mall on the Florence side of the Tennessee River. Terrell hired me to work at the store for my first job, and he exposed me to more musicians than I can count. He currently works as a tour guide at the old Muscle Shoals Sound Studio that has recently been renovated and reopened. All these years later, I still count Jay and Terrell among my closest friends.

DOWNTOWN FLORENCE, WHICH HAD BEEN FAST BECOMING A GHOST TOWN IN MY YOUTH, IS BEAUTIFUL AND REVITALIZED. MORE AND MORE YOUNG PEOPLE ARE FORMING BANDS AND HAVE A SENSE OF PRIDE IN MY HOMETOWN

My dad was never rich from his work as a session player, but we were comfortably upper-middle-class in a blue-collar town with a struggling economy. We lived in a neighborhood of older families, so I didn't have many kids my age to play with on my street. At school, I was far more interested in writing my songs than participating in sports, so I was frequently bullied by the other kids. By high school I had found close friends and I also grew six inches in one summer, so the bullying stopped. We built a house out on Shoals Creek [also known as Shoal Creek], and my high school years were generally fun.

As tensions from the civil rights era calmed down, my dad's work became less secretive, although I think most of the townsfolk were still somewhat oblivious to it all. Q107 might mention that a song they played was recorded there, but I'm not sure that actually registered with most of the people listening in their cars on their way to work, going about their lives. This probably explains how people as world famous as Mick Jagger, Bob Dylan, or Rod Stewart could stay at our local Holiday Inn and slip in and out basically undetected.

In 1982, the same month that I graduated from Coffee High School, the Ford plant announced that it would be closing. This began a domino effect that wrecked our hometown economy so bad that it has taken decades for it to rebuild. At about the same time, trends in music changed enough to essentially shut down the majority of our local recording scene. Many of the top session players moved north to

Nashville or west to L.A. seeking greener pastures and better gigs. My dad was one of the holdouts who stayed behind to try to keep it going in Muscle Shoals.

By the time I dropped out of college and began playing full time in my own band, the recording scene at home was dying off. As a dry county, we never had a live music scene other than a few cover bands playing Top 40 or country hits at one of the rough-and-tumble bars up at the Tennessee state line. When voters finally approved legal liquor sales, I had visions of a live music scene starting up like the celebrated one in Athens, Georgia, that was spawning bands like R.E.M. and the B-52's. Instead, we basically just got the same bars from the state line opening up in town. It was a dismal place to try to operate a punk band that only played the songs I was writing.

I moved away in the early '90s, eventually settling in Athens, where I was able to form the band that I still play in today. More and more young people left for better opportunities elsewhere. My dad and the other holdouts who refused to move away stayed on, doing the best they could amongst fewer and fewer bookings.

A few years ago, a couple of filmmakers, Greg Camalier and Stephen Badger, made *Muscle Shoals*, a documentary about the musical miracles that occurred there. It was a critical and commercial success and helped spark a renaissance of interest in this unique music scene. The film release coincided with a loosening up of restrictions from the local governments that enabled more new local music venues to exist.

Downtown Florence, which had been fast becoming a ghost town in my youth, is beautiful and revitalized. More and more young people are forming bands and have a sense of pride in my hometown—one I never could have imagined growing up. In 2015, Lincoln Center hosted a Muscle Shoals tribute show that drew thousands of fans.

My dad turned 77 this September. He is thankfully in great health and still plays at a level comparable to his prime. He was never a fancy type of player, he didn't "solo" or "thump" like some of his more flashy peers from the funk era. His signature is far more subtle, a matter of tone, of which he is considered a master, a melodicism in his playing that combines with a sort of minimalism to give him his unique and special sound. His Muscle Shoals sound.

I never played music with my father growing up. Whether it was a form of rebellion or just the times I came of age in, I gravitated toward a more unhinged and less disciplined sound in my own music. My early years as a player were spent trying to replicate a sound I heard in my head and to play the songs I was writing, and my dad often thought I was misguided in my early attempts at being a professional musician. Even though we both have the same basic occupation, we've always been on very different sides of it, and it wasn't until much later that we began to bridge that gap musically.

In more recent years, my dad has played on two of my solo albums and has sat in with my band on stage in some wonderful venues, including the legendary Fox Theatre in Atlanta. I played with my dad at premieres of the Muscle Shoals documentary in New York City and Seattle as well as the Muscle Shoals tribute at Lincoln Center in 2015. We also formed a band called Dickinsons + Hoods with legendary producer/keyboardist Jim Dickinson and his sons Luther and Cody [of the acclaimed and wonderful band North Mississippi Allstars] back in 2007. Jim passed away before we could complete the album we started, but last year we finally completed tracking it and hope to put it out in the next year.

Both FAME and the original Muscle Shoals Sound Studio are open for recording and as tourist destinations, complete with guides. The past few years have seen thousands of visitors from nearly every continent touring those tiny studios. With their mid-century furnishings and accompanying color schemes, they still look exactly as they did in the late '60s. And a new generation of musicians from the surrounding area is coming up—artists like Jason Isbell, Alabama Shakes, Dylan LeBlanc, and the Secret Sisters, as well as my own band Drive-By Truckers. I suspect there will be more to come, all of us staking our own claims to musical immortality.

PATTERSON HOOD is a writer, musician, songwriter and producer living in Portland, Oregon. He is originally from Muscle Shoals, Alabama, and plays in his band Drive-By Truckers as well as being a solo artist. This essay first appeared in *Oxford American*, November 2020.

TWO POEMS

Written by **ASHLEY M. JONES**

SAM COOKE SINGS TO ME WHEN I AM AFRAID

Sam Cooke plays on the cassette deck in our Nissan Sentra. I am strapped like a parachuter in my booster seat. It is Saturday night. We are travelling from grandma's house in Bessemer, having waited until the night's third episode of "Walker, Texas Ranger" to leave for home. I am scared because I am not touching my mother. Sam Cooke is crooning about a party or a lost love or a change coming, and I'm afraid to die. Tonight, Alabama doesn't feel like home—it is too dark to see and the alleys beckon our little car to them. Dad knows all the shortcuts because he's a fireman, and I wish so hard for the interstate with lights and its fast, homeward promise. I wish for our little home and all my toys, even the ones that scare me at night. I wish for morning, when I will eat collard greens and cornbread with Mom. I wish for playtime with Monique and our blue couch that is a jungle, that is Pride Rock, that is a spaceship. Sam Cooke is painfully singing. He's screaming. I can barely breathe behind all these straps—I am straightjacketed and trying to understand the hurt in Sam Cooke's voice, and why does grandma never get up from her easy chair? Why does she look out at us like we are this night—like we arc something she will never quite touch? Even when she laughs, why does she still look sad? Why have we not made it home yet? If I close my eyes and reach for sleep, can I make us teleport home? Sam Cooke, give me the answers instead of your steely wail.

GOD SPEAKS TO ALABAMA

I molded you
from red clay, sweet cornbread,
the slow drip of a lemon
squeezed over sugar and ice.
I kissed you to life, on the lips.
Mama bird I am—
my tongue feeds you blood.
I have waited
in this heat for you
to pucker
and say my name—
Hallelujah, Alabama.
I give you fire
and blackberries
and white, thick cotton.
I give you the honeybee
and the yellowhammer—
find me, swallow me down
and whisper me
to passerby
as you sit, nightly,
on the creaky
front porch.

ASHLEY M. JONES is the poet laureate of the state of Alabama (2022-2026). The poems here appear in her book, *Magic City Gospel* (Hub City Press, 2017), a love letter to Birmingham. She also is author of *dark / / thing* (Pleiades Press, 2019) and *REPARATIONS NOW!* (Hub City Press, 2021). She teaches in the Creative Writing Department of the Alabama School of Fine Arts, and she is part of the core faculty of the Converse University low residency MFA program.

IN SEARCH OF FOLK ART

Written by **AARON SANDERS HEAD**

I'VE LIVED NEARLY ALL MY LIFE IN ALABAMA. I've spent what surely amounts to years driving back roads, living by two rules: stop at every cemetery, and pull over if I see any yard art.

Yard art—one variety of a wildly diverse kind of creative expression generally known as "folk art"—was once more prevalent in Alabama. Artists like George Kornegay and Emmer Sewell filled their outdoor spaces with found-object testaments to their spirituality and prophetic warnings to passersby, like Kornegay's crosses and angels forged from chrome hubcaps and salvaged wood. Just west of Greensboro, in the even smaller community of Forkland, dotting the pasture off Highway 43, the yard art of the late Jim Bird teems with irregularly shaped hay bales and other farm detritus, including a 32-foot-tall tin man.

Bird's initial goal was to offer excitement to a vacant stretch of highway. Which is exactly what folk art does—take a seemingly unremarkable place and inject it with vitality, showing what happens when we use our environment as inspiration.

When folks ask about living in Alabama, its rambling legacy of folk art—sometimes also known as "outsider art" because its creators often work outside the mainstream art world of museums and galleries—swells me most with pride. Other states can borrow Gee's Bend quilts and Thornton Dial sculptures, but those wonders are eternally linked to the cultural landscape of my home state, born of brilliant minds that call Alabama home.

This type of art resists strict terminology—"folk," "outsider" and "visionary" are all terms one hears. But most broadly, "folk art" refers to artists who are self-taught. These are people who feel unfettered by convention, acting more as alchemists than artists. Folk art offers an expanded vision of possibility and can shift a viewer toward a sense of wonder. Through this lens, every experience seems an occasion for inspiration, and everyone has the capacity to be transported by the vision of these makers.

The most powerful way to experience this artwork is to be fully immersed in it, so I set off on a road trip in search of this Alabama legacy.

* * *

I started in my home of Greensboro, a rural town located in Hale County that boasts its own mystique, having been explored extensively by photographers William Christenberry and Walker Evans, and more recently by RaMell Ross. Southeast of Greensboro and Forkland are some of the most famous cultural touchstones of Alabama—the quilts made in the community of Gee's Bend, largely by women.

I like to reach Gee's Bend by car, or more directly by taking the ferry from nearby Camden. The ferry has a sordid history. It was discontinued during the 1960s battle for civil rights to prevent the politically active Gee's Bend citizens from registering to vote. Today, though, the ferry is electric and takes just 15 minutes. The ferry terminal is near the Gee's Bend Welcome Center, where visitors can view quilts and meet quilters. As I drive the winding river roads of Boykin, I'm reminded of the time I visited for Gee's Bend's Airing of the Quilts, a soul-stirring event now held annually in early October. For decades, when the first bit of cold is felt, families in Gee's Bend have pulled out their quilts and hung them on fences, clotheslines and hillsides to air them out. Seeing these tableaus dotted with multicolored textile masterpieces is surreal. When you see Minnie Sue Coleman's quilts hanging on a fence she built herself, you realize how tied to the land these works are—rectangles inspired by shacks, lines that evoke pine trees, stitches that echo the bend of the river.

Often created from clothing or scraps from commercial sewing gigs, these explosively colorful quilts pivot from restrained minimalism to indulgent textured wonderland. And while they have taken the art world by storm in recent years—a major 2002 show at The Museum of Fine Arts, Houston, then traveled to the Whitney Museum of American Art and other major institutions—Gee's Bend has developed a visual language for far longer. Quilting tradition here stretches back beyond the 19th century.

Gee's Bend, officially known as Boykin, is a small area bordered on three sides by the Alabama River. Boykin is the site of a former plantation, with many current residents directly related to the formerly enslaved population. Much of the attention given to Gee's Bend focuses on its seclusion and poverty—there's often an implied sense of surprise that this incredible work could be created in such a place. Perhaps it would be more fair and illuminating to focus on the brilliant talents of Black women, who developed an unrivaled style.

These works celebrate the traditions that hold rural communities together. Gee's Bend taught me from a young age that you can make studied, abstract work about your home, and that revelation changed the entire course of my life. When these works hang in the place that inspired them, the realm of regional expression feels infinite.

* * *

A few hours south of Gee's Bend along 43 I take in an entirely new landscape. First, a swamp that folks have tried to tame with concrete. Then, the Gulf Coast, where nature takes back full control in the Mobile Bay. I start at Callaghan's Irish Social Club, where Abe Partridge, a former Baptist preacher and current folk artist and musician, is playing to a devoted audience. Mobile is Abe's home. He first started painting during a difficult stint as a pastor and then steered his work in a more personal direction. After much experimentation, Abe landed on a time-intensive process. First, he spreads a layer of tar on panels that cure for several weeks. He then carves into and paints that tar to depict snake-handlers and rock-and-rollers, an appropriate mixture of his spiritual and creative lives.

One notable piece depicts a man with a candlestick perched on his outstretched tongue and a head full of flowers, with scrawled text reminding you to "take care of the weeds on yr head before you worry about the ones in yr field." It would be easy to peg this kind of raw expression as a thing of the past in Alabama. But Abe, a relatively young man in the thick of his creative career, points toward a fertile future. The same is to be said for Charlie "The Tin Man" Lucas, who continues in his 70s to make vital work at his studio in downtown

Selma, where he loves visitors. Or Butch Anthony and his Museum of Wonder in Seale, Alabama, where visitors can take in a drive-through museum or catch a tour of Butch's studio to see a glimpse into his world full of taxidermy, bones, trophies and embroidered paintings.

* * *

Even so, many folk artists are only remembered through historic markers. In 2019, one such roadside monument was erected on the corner of Monroe and North Lawrence in downtown Montgomery, where Bill Traylor, a preeminent folk artist, created thousands of paintings between 1939 and 1942. Born into enslavement and later living as a sharecropper, Traylor moved to Montgomery at the age of 75. There, he began obsessively painting scenes of the city's downtown and harrowing memories of enslaved life, creating one of the most powerful visual lexicons in all of self-taught art. These works are complex observations—an attempt to carve out an identity in a modernizing world still steeped in racism. Being able to stand in the spot where a brilliant man fearlessly chronicled a rapidly changing world is a powerful thing.

North of Montgomery in Prattville, not far from Highway 65, I arrive at W.C. Rice's Cross Garden. Born in 1930, Rice was a house painter and born-again Christian who devoted his art to God after recovering from a stomach illness—he attributed his return to health to divine healing. Rice created hundreds of crosses, emblazoned with fire-and-brimstone phrasings: SEX KILLS; HELL IS HOT HOT HOT. He devoted his house to his work and then quickly filled his 3 acres with refrigerators, washing machines and all kinds of metal—all marked with Rice's proclamations of the dangers of immorality.

Rice died in 2004, and each year the garden loses a few crosses to the kudzu, which will eventually fully reclaim it. I always find myself pulled here, a magnetism felt despite a difference in faith, compelled by the way the place enables me to see what the world looks like to a man who feels changed by a higher force, and his compulsion to share that with those around him.

About 80 miles north of Prattville, we find Joe Minter's African Village in America, one of the only remaining folk "environments" in Birmingham. This rarity informs the viewing of Joe Minter's sprawling creation, located in a fenced area on a dead-end street in South Birmingham. Joe's body of work consists of found-object sculptures and recreations of civil rights locations, like Martin Luther King Jr.'s jail cell.

One might hear a stir somewhere deep in the jumble of materials here. It's likely Joe, trimming weeds or working on a new piece. Joe often ventures to City Hall, setting up his work on the steps to voice his concerns; signs at his property advertise a self-tour policy if he's gone. The property adjoins two historically Black cemeteries, and Minter says he feels those souls around him, calling out for recognition. Using scraps of the industries that built Birmingham, Minter has created a memorial to people of color who created the city, even while it excluded them. In his 1995 piece *Four Hundred Years of Free Labor*, Minter welds together rakes, shovels and spades covered in heavy chains, commemorating the enslaved laborers who came before him.

The work is both uneasy and exuberant—an appropriate depiction of life in Alabama—and it is difficult to leave the world Joe Minter has built without feeling an internal shift and a rebuilding of the legacy of a complicated region.

* * *

North of Birmingham in Cullman, nestled into the grounds of St. Bernard Abbey, we find Ave Maria Grotto, the life's work of Brother Joseph Zoettl, a Benedictine monk at the abbey for almost 70 years. In the 1930s Zoettl began creating miniatures of historic religious sites from around the world using an assortment of found objects, now housed in a shaded park with a winding two-block-long pathway pulling you through 125 mixed-media sculptures. The works include a miniature Tower of Babel, complete with wrecking ball, as well as a miniature Jerusalem. The centerpiece is the giant Ave Maria Grotto itself, standing a staggering 27 feet tall and 27 feet deep, adorned with cement crosses and religious sculptures.

Walking through this deeply weird, deeply beautiful environment, there's a sense of arrival. Maybe folk art can't really be said to have one center, capital or home. But this is a place defined by untamed imagination. As I drive these roads again, I'm reminded that there is always something to the initial act of discovery. The best part of

this artistic landscape is that there are undiscovered visionary artists working right now in rural Alabama, contributing to the complex tapestry of what it means to live creatively. Will those artists be discovered? Do they want to be found? What is clear is that there's an ineffable quality to Alabama that compels its people to create. The state's roads can take you into their brilliant works and imaginations.

AARON SANDERS HEAD is an Alabama-based textile artist whose work explores the lived experiences of rural Alabamians. His learned sense of observation combined with inherited family traditions of textile and agriculture inform the unique visual language Aaron works in today, which exists in the worlds of quiltmaking, handwork, mending and natural dyes..

DIRECTORY & INDEX

DIRECTORY

MUSIC SITES

Alabama Music Box, *Mobile*
Alabama Music Hall of Fame, *Tuscumbia*
Alabama Theatre, *Birmingham*
Avondale Brewing Company, *Birmingham*
Callaghan's Irish Social Club, *Mobile*
Dauphin Street Sound, *Mobile*
FAME Recording Studios, *Muscle Shoals*
Hank Williams Museum & Gravesite, *Montgomery*
Lava Room, *Florence*
Lyric Theatre, *Birmingham*
Muscle Shoals Sound Studio, *Sheffield*
The Nick, *Birmingham*
The NuttHouse, *Sheffield*
Oak Mountain Amphitheatre, *Pelham*
The Orion Amphitheater, *Huntsville*
Saturn, *Birmingham*
Standard Deluxe, *Waverly*
Sun Ra's grave, *Birmingham*
Three Caves, *Huntsville*
W.C. Handy Birthplace, Museum and Library, *Florence*
Wishbone Recording Studio, *Muscle Shoals*

NATURAL WORLD

Audubon Bird Sanctuary, *Dauphin Island*
Birmingham Botanical Gardens, *Birmingham*
Blakeley State Park, *Spanish Fort*
Cahaba River, *Jefferson County*
Cathedral Caverns, *Woodville*
Cheaha State Park, *Delta*
The Cold Hole, *Magnolia Springs*
Cypress Creek, *Florence*
Dauphin Island Sea Lab, *Dauphin Island*
DeSoto State Park, *Fort Payne*
Dothan Area Botanical Gardens, *Dothan*
Gulf State Park, *Gulf Shores*
Lake Guntersville State Park, *Guntersville*
Little River Canyon, *Fort Payne*
Manitou Cave, *Fort Payne*
Monte Sano State Park, *Huntsville*
Moundville Archaeological Park, *Moundville*
Oak Mountain State Park, *Pelham*
Old Cahawba Archaeological Park, *Orrville*
Railroad Park, *Birmingham*
Red Mountain Park, *Birmingham*
Wheeler & Wilson lakes, *The Shoals*
Wichahpi Commemorative Stone Wall [*Tom's Wall*], *Florence*

PLATE LUNCHES

Archibald's, *Northport*
Big Bob Gibston Bar-B-Q, *Decatur*
Bob Sykes Bar-B-Q, *Bessemer*
Bunyan's Bar-B-Que, *Florence*
Byron's Smokehouse, *Auburn*
Demetri's BBQ, *Homewood*
Dreamland Bar-B-Que, *Tuscaloosa*
Eagle's Restaurant, *Birmingham*
Golden Rule Bar-B-Q and Grill, *Irondale*
Johnny's Restaurant, *Homewood*
Kalim Korean BBQ, *Montgomery*
Lannie's Bar-B-Q Spot, *Selma*
Mary's Southern Cooking, *Mobile*
Niki's West, *Birmingham*
Ted's Restaurant, *Birmingham*
The Bright Star, *Bessemer*

INDEX